Praise for *The Elephant in the Boardroom*

"This practical book should be in the hands of every pastor and board chair. It provides the right answer to one of the most neglected areas of church life today—effective leadership transition in the local church."

— Dr. William O. (Bill) Crews, chancellor, Golden Gate
   Baptist Theological Seminary, Mill Valley, California

"Choosing a CEO is probably the most important thing a corporate board does. The church is no different. This book helps elevate the priority and process of properly choosing a new senior pastor. All congregations would benefit from this book."

— Terry Looper, chairman and CEO,
   Texon Holding, Houston, Texas

"Practical advice for a critical problem. The authors' explanation of strategic planning and organizational culture is worth the price of the book."

— Rev. Gary DeLashmutt, lead pastor,
   Xenos Christian Fellowship, Columbus, Ohio

"Crabtree and Weese expose the huge costs and avoidable causes of poor pastoral transitions. They offer a wise strategy to prepare for the inevitable leadership changes every church will face."

— Dr. George K. Brushaber, president,
   Bethel College and Seminary, St. Paul, Minnesota

The Elephant in the Boardroom

Speaking the Unspoken About Pastoral Transitions

Carolyn Weese

J. Russell Crabtree

A LEADERSHIP ❖ NETWORK PUBLICATION

JOSSEY-BASS
A Wiley Imprint
www.josseybass.com

Published by Jossey-Bass
A Wiley Imprint
989 Market Street, San Francisco, CA 94103-1741   www.josseybass.com

Jossey-Bass books and products are available through most bookstores. To contact Jossey-Bass
directly call our Customer Care Department within the U.S. at 800-956-7739, outside the
U.S. at 317-572-3986, or fax 317-572-4002.

Jossey-Bass also publishes its books in a variety of electronic formats. Some content that
appears in print may not be available in electronic books.

Library of Congress Cataloging-in-Publication Data

Weese, Carolyn, date.
   The elephant in the boardroom : speaking the unspoken about pastoral transitions /
Carolyn Weese, J. Russell Crabtree.
      p. cm.
   Includes index.
   ISBN 978-0-7879-7257-8 (alk. paper)
   1. Pastoral theology. 2. Clergy—Office. I. Crabtree, J. Russell, date. II. Title.
   BV4011.3.W44 2004
   253—dc22   2004002664

Printed in the United States of America
FIRST EDITION
HB Printing   10 9 8 7 6 5 4 3

Other Leadership Network Titles

The Blogging Church: Sharing the Story of Your Church Through Blogs, by Brian Bailey and Terry Storch

Leading from the Second Chair: Serving Your Church, Fulfilling Your Role, and Realizing Your Dreams, by Mike Bonem and Roger Patterson

The Way of Jesus: A Journey of Freedom for Pilgrims and Wanderers, by Jonathan S. Campbell with Jennifer Campbell

Leading the Team-Based Church: How Pastors and Church Staffs Can Grow Together into a Powerful Fellowship of Leaders, by George Cladis

Organic Church: Growing Faith Where Life Happens, by Neil Cole

Off-Road Disciplines: Spiritual Adventures of Missional Leaders, by Earl Creps

Leading Congregational Change Workbook, by James H. Furr, Mike Bonem, and Jim Herrington

Leading Congregational Change: A Practical Guide for the Transformational Journey, by Jim Herrington, Mike Bonem, and James H. Furr.

The Leader's Journey: Accepting the Call to Personal and Congregational Transformation, by Jim Herrington, Robert Creech, and Trisha Taylor

Culture Shift: Transforming Your Church from the Inside Out, by Robert Lewis and Wayne Cordeiro, with Warren Bird

A New Kind of Christian: A Tale of Two Friends on a Spiritual Journey, by Brian D. McLaren

The Story We Find Ourselves In: Further Adventures of a New Kind of Christian, by Brian D. McLaren

Practicing Greatness: 7 Disciplines of Extraordinary Spiritual Leaders, by Reggie McNeal

The Present Future: Six Tough Questions for the Church, by Reggie McNeal

A Work of Heart: Understanding How God Shapes Spiritual Leaders, by Reggie McNeal

The Millennium Matrix: Reclaiming the Past, Reframing the Future of the Church, by M. Rex Miller

Shaped by God's Heart: The Passion and Practices of Missional Churches, by Milfred Minatrea

The Ascent of a Leader: How Ordinary Relationships Develop Extraordinary Character and Influence, by Bill Thrall, Bruce McNicol, and Ken McElrath

The Missional Leader: Equipping Your Church to Reach a Changing World, by Alan J. Roxburgh and Fred Romanuk

The Elephant in the Boardroom: Speaking the Unspoken About Pastoral Transitions, by Carolyn Weese and J. Russell Crabtree

Contents

List of Exhibits

About Leadership Network

SINCE 1984, Leadership Network has fostered church innovation and growth by diligently pursuing its far-reaching mission statement: to identify, connect, and help high-capacity Christian leaders multiply their impact.

Although Leadership Network's techniques adapt and change as the church faces new opportunities and challenges, the organization's work follows a consistent and proven pattern: Leadership Network brings together entrepreneurial leaders who are focused on similar ministry initiatives. The ensuing collaboration—often across denominational lines—creates a strong base from which individual leaders can better analyze and refine their own strategies. Peer-to-peer interaction, dialogue, and sharing inevitably accelerate participants' innovation and ideas. Leadership Network further enhances this process through developing and distributing highly targeted ministry tools and resources, including audio and video programs, special reports, e-publications, and online downloads.

With Leadership Network's assistance, today's Christian leaders are energized, equipped, inspired, and better able to multiply their own dynamic Kingdom-building initiatives.

Launched in 1996 in conjunction with Jossey-Bass (a Wiley imprint), Leadership Network Publications present thoroughly researched and innovative concepts from leading thinkers, practitioners, and pioneering churches. The series collectively draws from a range of disciplines, with individual titles offering perspective on one or more of five primary areas:

1. Enabling effective leadership
2. Encouraging life-changing service
3. Building authentic community
4. Creating Kingdom-centered impact
5. Engaging cultural and demographic realities

For additional information on the mission or activities of Leadership Network, please contact:

Leadership Network
(800) 765–5323
client.care@leadnet.org

Preface

For more than twenty years, we have been consulting with, researching, and surveying hundreds of churches of all denominations, sizes, locations, and theological persuasions. During that time, we have seen many changes, some of them heartening and others not so encouraging. One aspect has been consistent across all these churches: they do not plan for the inevitable moment when their current pastor leaves. Given the intimate connection between a congregation's morale and its pastor's worship leadership, we were troubled when we saw that most churches do not have a plan in place to sustain excellence and continuity in succession planning. Writers in the business and leadership world have dealt extensively with the subject, but there are no foundational concepts for handling it successfully in the church world.

With this book, we offer a resource that is both practical and inspirational. It is born of the hope that by helping people face their fears and at the same time provide them with a quality resource, churches will be better able to make a successful transition from one leader to another. We are challenging the reader to think outside the box and grasp new concepts for healthy pastoral transitions. It is our prayer that this book will break the silence about the elephant in the church boardroom and guide clergy and lay leaders, drawing them together to pray, discuss, and plan for pastoral changes that sustain excellence of ministry at the time of a leadership transition.

June 2004

Carolyn Weese
Russ Crabtree

To the Crabtree Family
Emily, Mark, Sarah, Elizabeth, and Michael

And to the Weese Family
Harvey, Karen, Jim, Austin, and Taylor

Acknowledgments

Though a book may be penned by one or two hands, there lies behind the writing a company of people who have provided insight, guidance, support, wisdom, life experience, encouragement, and much more. As two explorers on a journey into the wilderness of succession planning in the church, we found we were charting a course rather than following an already prescribed direction. Our experiences in the church over the past twenty years have shaped much of who we are and what we have written. Acknowledging all of the churches, pastors, and people who contributed to our thinking is impossible. However, it is important to mention a few names. Linda Karlovec was a constant source of insight. Leta Cook and Vicki Rush, as friends and church workers, offered continual encouragement. Harvey Weese would not allow us to lose the dream for this book and patiently endured the long days of collaboration.

We also express a special word of appreciation to David G. McKechnie (pastor) and Terry Looper (elder) of Grace Presbyterian Church, Houston, Texas, for catching the vision with us while it was in its infant stage and encouraging us to move forward with the project. We deeply appreciate the very special part they played in making this book possible. Dan Klein, of Texas Presbyterian Foundation, caught the vision for the book as well and spread it among his colleagues.

When we first discussed the possibility of such a book with Carol Childress, of Leadership Network, she responded enthusiastically.

Her constant support for the project confirmed that we did have a story that needed to be told.

Last, but certainly not least, without God's help it would not have been written. According to His plan, calendars were opened to make time available, funding was furnished, and two colleagues successfully narrowed the space between Ohio and Arizona in order to collaborate on the work. To God be the glory!

The Elephant in the Boardroom

Introduction

> I have no greater joy than to hear that my children
> are walking in the truth.
>
> —3 John 1:4 (NIV)

The fact that you have picked up this book and begun to read it says something about you. You are probably a leader in the church, lay or pastor, and are likely a think-outside-the-box leader. What you may be thinking about in this season of your life is one of the most important questions you will have to tackle as a leader: pastoral transition. How you handle this question determines whether or not you will have the greatest joy of which John speaks, a strong legacy of faith in the lives of those you have led. Whether pastor or lay leader, think for a moment about these questions:

- Do you have a strategic plan that defines where your church is going and how you are going to get there?
- Do you have a clear understanding of your particular church culture and the specific advantages and risks posed to that culture by a pastoral transition?
- Have you had an honest, structured discussion with your governing board about what is going to happen to the church when the pastor leaves?
- Does your governing board have a clear, Biblically based, shared understanding of the spiritual principles that should inform a pastoral transition process?
- Do you have a pastoral transition plan in place that describes in detail how your church will maintain excellence at the point when the current pastor leaves and a new pastor is called?

- Do you have a crisis plan in place, should something happen that requires the pastor to leave suddenly?

- Have you identified in advance the consultant resources you will need in order to make a successful pastoral transition, and have you made sure they have a proven track record of effectiveness? This includes denominational agencies serving as consultants.

- Has your governing board calculated all the various costs that would be associated with a poorly managed pastoral transition?

If you are like the large majority of church leaders in the United States, your answer to most of these questions is no. When it comes to dealing with a pastoral transition, many strong leaders stop leading, and it is likely that they are heading toward a story that may sound familiar to you.

The Story of Meadowbrook Church

This is a story about a pastor named Pete. Pete was a good pastor and a great guy. He served Meadowbrook Church for ten years, and the church grew to about twice as big as it was when he came. One day Pete decided that the Lord wanted him to move on to another church. Now, Pete wanted to do this right, and doing it right meant making sure that *no one at Meadowbrook knew he was thinking of leaving.* On the day he decided that the Lord wanted him to move, Pete realized he would have to live a double life. This was a change, because generally speaking Pete was a person of integrity. He was about to live a part of his life in secrecy.

He went on living the life he had lived for ten years at Meadowbrook, the one that everyone had come to know and appreciate. But secretly Pete was living a second life off the radar screen. He was praying for a new call. He was talking to his family about moving. He was scheduling secret meetings after worship with strangers who had come to hear him preach. He was telling people he was off on vacation when he was really looking at other churches. He was having his mail sent to his home rather than to the church, and he set up a separate e-mail account with its own password.

Pete was incredible as a secret agent pastor. He was able to live these two separate lives for a full eight months. He baptized babies, prayed for the sick, ran board meetings, and preached great sermons (many of which he secretly duplicated to send to other churches). Not a single person at Meadowbrook caught on to the other life that Pete was leading behind the scenes.

The phone rang one day, bringing news of a call to Riverton Church. Pete scheduled a meeting with the Meadowbrook board, announcing that he would be leaving in three weeks. One party (a real gush-and-blow), five speeches, and ten boxes of Kleenex later, Pete was gone. As he drove his family across three states to their new home, he thought, *I did it! I was a secret agent pastor for eight months. And no one figured it out!*

Three blocks away from Meadowbrook lived a woman named Betty. She was on the board, and for about eight months she had been worrying about what would happen to the church if Pastor Pete ever left. But Betty didn't say anything because she knew that even if Pete was thinking of leaving, he was not supposed to tell anyone. Like Pete, Betty did it "right." She sat through eight months of board meetings holding her tongue. All the time she voted, debated, and prayed on the outside, she was worrying and fretting on the inside. Betty was not talking about the most important concern on her mind.

For Pete, Betty, and other board members, this was the *elephant in the boardroom*. It was big. It was threatening. And everyone acted as if it weren't there.

One week after Pete left, Betty sat at a board meeting where people were trying to figure out what to do next. No one had a clue where to find a person to provide temporary pastoral services, so they ended up hiring a retired minister just to fill the pulpit during the search process.

Three weeks later, Betty was trying to understand the process for finding a new minister and learned that it would take about eighteen months.

Eight weeks later, Betty was at a board meeting where they received the resignation of the youth minister.

Ten weeks later she received the resignation letter of the associate pastor, who was afraid that she might not fit in with a new pastor.

Three months later, Betty and the board were looking at worship attendance figures that had dropped 20 percent since Pete's departure.

Four months later, Betty and the board were trying to figure out where to cut the budget in order to get through the rest of the year because giving had fallen off.

Six months later, Betty learned that two board members had resigned and were attending another church.

Eight months later, Betty heard that the search committee had a candidate ready to meet the board.

Nine months later, Betty learned that the candidate had changed his mind and wanted a larger church.

Ten months later Betty started getting angry phone calls from members that the process was taking too long.

Finally, a *year and a half* after Pastor Pete left, Pastor John began at Meadowbrook Church. Betty said to herself, *We did it. We survived the loss of Pastor Pete.*

When the new pastor arrived, he wanted to do things his own way. So he changed Sunday worship from 11:00 A.M. to 10:30 A.M. and added a guitar. No one told him that the top three givers in the church didn't believe in pledging, or that they golfed together every Tuesday. When he preached a stewardship sermon about the evils of uncommitted members who refuse to pledge, he promptly lost about $60,000 of income in the church. And because he didn't know that the lay leader's daughter had died by suicide five years earlier, when he preached a sermon about suicide being a self-centered act he lost two families in less than a week.

Betty began to get phone calls regularly from members wondering why the new pastor was so out of touch with his members.

Church land is filled with good pastors like Pete, and good board members like Betty, who don't talk about the most important event that can happen to their church—the elephant in the boardroom, or call it pastoral transition. Because they didn't talk about it, everyone suffered. Pete sacrificed some of his integrity to live a double life. The board was thrust into a church crisis without a clue or forethought about what to do next. Pastor John stepped into a good church with a few land mines. Pete had known all about those land mines, but the new pastor stumbled onto and exploded them. The congregation felt betrayed by a process that left them weakened, diminished, and demoralized. On and on it goes.

Today, many churches talk about and develop some form of a strategic plan that they attempt to live into over a period of several years. Most often, those plans contain information about the renovation or building of facilities. They include financial information about budget and endowment funds and talk about the need to increase stewardship. A strategic plan also discusses the direction and expansion of ministries, and how those ministries will be staffed. But—too often—nowhere does a strategic plan discuss the particulars of preparing for a time when the present pastor will no longer be the senior pastor of the church. Succession planning is the second most important need in every church in the country (well-trained and committed pastoral and lay leadership that is culturally relevant being the first), and few if any do it or do it well.

Pastoral Transitions That Fit the Church of Today

This book is for today. Unfortunately, we often operate out of a church paradigm that worked fifty years ago. In that era of high denominational loyalty, transitions were much less disorienting owing to off-the-shelf ministry approaches universally applied, simple programmatic paths to success (worship, Sunday school, youth group), an ample supply of ministers, and low mobility among church members. People tended to stay with a church through its transition, and the new pastor from Seattle used the same curriculum as the former pastor from Bloomington.

Today, ministry is much more localized, customized, specialized, and complex. What works in Seattle may not work in Bloomington. The high-stress culture in which we all swim is not one in which many people can survive a long period of tumult in their primary resource for emotional and spiritual stability. They move on to another congregation.

This book calls us to imagine a transition process that fits the church of today rather than the one of fifty years ago. For a moment, imagine a church:

- That is so invested in its mission that it is willing not only to break the taboo and talk about leadership changes but also to manage them
- With a vision for excellence in managing leadership transitions
- Where leadership changes do not blindside or sidetrack the vision
- Where the vision manages change, rather than change managing the vision
- Where inspired leaders are insistent that the Body grow from strength to strength and from leader to leader, rather than from avoidance to chaos
- Where a clear, Biblically based plan is activated when leaders change
- Where veteran leaders mentor emerging leaders
- Where the specific gifts of the Body are called forth to manage transitions
- Where the sheep are not scattered by the wolf of denial and ambush but instead dwell in a confidence that is the fruit of studied readiness

The goal of this book is to move toward that kind of church.

For change to take place, we must recognize and honor the inner wisdom that guides people to do what they do. When intelligent, dedicated, God-loving, one-another-loving people sit together in a boardroom and choose not to talk about an issue that is so vital to everyone's well-being and obvious to everyone, they are not being obstinate or cowardly. They are responding to the feeling that they are not equipped to deal with the issue and that a poorly equipped foray into the unknown could make things worse.

Reshaping the leadership culture in churches to address the pastoral transition issues requires that people on both sides of the board table, lay and clergy, have tools that inspire confidence in a successful outcome. A workshop approach that equips one person on pastoral transitions and then requires him or her to market these ideas to restive fellows asks too much of both the individual and the culture. This book is intended for everyone in the boardroom. In fact, we strongly advise that every member read this book, before a board discusses this issue at any length.

What's in This Book for You?

The book begins, in Part One, by making a case for a different way of doing pastoral transitions. Chapter One lays the spiritual foundation for pastoral transitions by looking at how Jesus dealt with them in His own life, first as a successor to John the Baptist and then as the predecessor of the ministry of the disciples. Chapter Two looks at the costs of poorly managed pastoral transitions, costs that most people would agree are too high and demand a *metanoia* (changed mind). Closing Part One, Chapter Three discusses health-based pastoral transitions and how they differ from an illness-based model. The chapter also includes an important description of the key players in a healthy transition and the roles they play.

Part Two presents a model to explain how various church cultures respond to pastoral transitions. Chapter Four describes and names four cultures (a family culture, an icon culture, an archival culture, and a replication culture) and ends with a generic description of each culture to help the reader locate his or her church in the model. Chapters Five through Eight are devoted to each cultural type, with a fuller description of the ideas, vocabulary, and values found in each one. The transition characteristics of each type are defined, with attention to the advantages, risks, threats, tasks, strategies, and advance planning required in each one. At the end of Part Two, the reader should sense a greater understanding of a particular church culture and the salient issues of the culture that need to be addressed for a healthy transition.

Part Three looks at the larger issues that should be addressed in an effective transition plan. Chapter Nine considers strategic planning, its role in setting the specifications for the new pastor, and the various strategic considerations in transition planning itself. Chapter Ten introduces the concepts of *unique mission components* and *asset transfer*. Both concepts talk about what is strong and vital in the church and how to maintain them across a pastoral transition. Chapter Eleven considers the *bench strength* of a church in terms of its *capability and maturity*, with consideration given to the resiliency of the organization and the work of the new pastor in building on that strength. Chapter Twelve discusses pastoral transitions for low-performance churches. Part Three continues with Chapter Thirteen and a discussion about developing a *crisis transition plan*. Finally, Chapter Fourteen encourages the reader to get started by taking constructive steps to help bring about a sea change in how the church thinks about and deals with pastoral transitions.

We recommend that leaders read the entire book. However, in an age of cramped calendars and time constraints an abridgement might be to read Part One and skip to the appropriate church type in Part Two. Part Three could be left for those responsible for actually developing a transition plan.

Adult learning works best when new information can be immediately applied. At a minimum, we recommend that a crisis transition plan be developed for every church. This book is an excellent introduction to the topic and will get people engaged in the issue. In such a case, board members need to read only Chapters One through Four and Chapter Thirteen.

Throughout the text, we speak about the *board* of the church. This refers to the group of leaders who are generally the elected or appointed decision makers setting policy, direction, vision, and so on. It is often referred to as the session, vestry, council, coordinating committee, church board. We are ever mindful of the fact that women and men fill the pastoral and lay leadership roles in the church today; therefore we have tried to be inclusive throughout the text.

Lastly, to all of the pioneers who dare to explore pastoral transitions in today's church and have the courage to plan in advance for that certainty, we offer our blessings and trust that this will be a great adventure for all those involved.

Part One

The Principles, Cost, and Players in Health-Based Transition

Chapter One

Principles of Transition, Jesus Style

And this is my prayer: that your love may abound
more and more in knowledge and depth of
insight. . . .

—*Philippians 1:9 (NIV)*

We do not say it frequently in this book, but it is important to state emphatically that the personal and corporate spiritual work required in a successful pastoral transition is critical. It would be a mistake to interpret the organizational and managerial tone of this book as dismissive of that spiritual work. Linda Karlovec, a psychologist who specializes in organizational therapy, argues that almost all resistance to organizational change is emotional, *though it is perceived to be rational*. This implies that the entire pastoral-transition enterprise needs to include the spiritual components of prayer, Scripture reading, personal reflection, confession, and nurture of faith. The life, teaching, and prayers of Jesus constitute a particularly rich source of sustenance for this journey.

Transformation is not a function of information, but of exploration with trust. People must find enough strength in their relationship with God and their trust of one another to be able to talk openly, pray, confess, and seek grace and healing if they are to develop excellence in a leadership transition. The capacity of a leader, or a group of leaders, to face their own shadow side through the power of Jesus Christ is critical to effectiveness in succession planning.

It is difficult to imagine a man more insistent and articulate regarding His own leadership transitions than Jesus of Nazareth, as described in the record of the New Testament. At the beginning of His ministry, He is clear and unambiguous. In Luke 4:16 (NIV), He enters the synagogue in His home town, reads a passage from the prophet Isaiah, and unmistakably lays His hand to the reins of leadership: "Today these words are fulfilled in your hearing." At the end of His ministry, He is equally clear and unambiguous; in John 16:16 (NIV) Jesus says, "A little while and you will see me no more." Later, we delve into the spiritual principles that seemed to be guiding Jesus. For now, suffice it to say that Jesus was candid and forthright about His arrival on the scene and equally transparent regarding His departure. Although the people on both ends tried to deny this reality, Jesus was unrelenting in His focus.

In the church today, the situation is often reversed. Members try to face the reality of a leadership change, while the leader denies it. Members know that they are the ones who will be left to deal with the shock wave of a sudden departure, and all the aftershocks as well. But when they try to talk honestly about this, the leader often dismisses the concern with an ambiguous response concerning God's will, God's call, and God's timing. Leaders who design worship services with an impulse of excellence driving every detail are willing to leave the impact of a major leadership transition to a curious silence. When it comes to pastoral transition, leaders often stop leading.

Why? The reasons certainly cannot be traced to the behavior or the teaching of Jesus. Instead of being grounded in spiritual principle, the reasons for silence seem to be rooted more in fear and low self-confidence. We are afraid that:

- If we talk about pastoral transition we might put the idea in someone's head and make it more likely to happen.

- We will create a lame duck situation in which effective ministry becomes impossible.

- A discussion about pastoral transition will have unintended consequences that we do not know how to manage.
- We don't have the resources to deal with transition planning and be successful.
- Our peers and colleagues won't support us in doing it a different way, and we are not sure we want to be pioneers on the road of better pastoral transition if this means going it alone.

All these issues can be addressed given the right resources and spiritual resolve. At the present time, however, church culture in North America does not provide these resources. The end result is that the congregation is left with no alternative but to experience the triple whammy of emotional, "organic," and organizational change all at the same time. As a whole, the church is a living, breathing organism and experiences all of the same emotions as an individual. At the same time, it is also an institution that experiences change at an organizational level as well. Thus, the triple whammy.

Jesus Did It Differently

Choose a number between one and twenty. There are that many reasons why the church must manage leadership transitions in a different way. But the most compelling reason is as simple as it is basic: Jesus did it differently. It is fundamentally an issue of discipleship. How can we claim to be following Jesus, when our practice of managing leadership transition runs directly counter to the model of His life?

Unfortunately, the people who genuinely sound like Jesus on this issue are not in the church, but in business. During his last years of service, the CEO of a large corporation said that putting in place a succession plan was what he spent most of his time thinking about. In an important work on succession planning, one author argued that a good plan is needed to avoid undermining the entire transition process and creating lingering casualties. How many church leaders understand that the failure to manage their transition to another ministry with clarity and wisdom creates lingering casualties among the members they have worked so hard to cultivate? One of the long-term needs that human beings have is to leave a legacy. It is small comfort for a pastor to look back over a lifetime of service and see three or four seasons of dynamic ministry punctuated by decline and retrenchment after his or her departure because inadequate attention was given to a transition plan. Jesus' transition plan for His own disciples included a vision for long-term results: "You did not choose me, but I chose you and appointed you to go and bear fruit—fruit that will last" (John 15:16 NIV).

Jesus managed two major leadership transitions in His life. He managed His succession of His predecessor, and He managed His own departure. Today's leader has to manage these same transitions as well. But the impetus to do so requires understanding *management as an expression of discipleship*. The example of Jesus is rich and illuminating. We cannot derive specific transition strategies that would fit the multiplicity of church governments today, but certain *start-up principles* emerge that apply across the spectrum of churches.

Principle One: Honor Thy Predecessor

Practically, honoring our predecessor means we should use TLC with members regarding a predecessor. That's *talk*, *listen*, and *confirm*.

Leaders help the transition process if they simply *talk* about their predecessor. Jesus did. He talked about John the Baptist on multiple occasions in public settings. Here is a list of some things Jesus said about His predecessor in public:

> Among those born of women, there has not arisen anyone greater than John . . . (Matthew 11:11 NIV)
>
> For John came to show you the way of righteousness . . . (Matthew 21:32 NIV)
>
> For John came neither eating bread nor drinking wine, and you say, he has a demon. (Luke 7:33 NIV)
>
> The baptism of John—was it from heaven or from men? (Mark 11:30 NIV)

Jesus was not afraid to talk about His predecessor *in public*. Yet many church members experience an eerie silence on the part of their new pastor regarding the work of his or her predecessor. It would be refreshing and liberating for many members to hear their pastor speak, in positive terms, the name of the pastor who went before and was referred to as an instrument in God's plan for building that church. In reality, the opposite is often the case. A pastor is sometimes so threatened by the esteem paid to a predecessor that he or she gives the signal to members that they are not to speak about the predecessor in the pastor's presence.

This leads to *listening*. Members need leaders to listen to them talk about their affection for their predecessor. This enables them to integrate their past and present experiences rather than compartmentalize them. If the leader is unwilling to do this, it places an emotional burden on the members. In one church, members made an agreement with one another not to speak the name of a former pastor except in private for nearly twenty years after the pastor left the community and moved to another state!

Ken Blanchard, of *One Minute Manager* fame, said that "what we resist, persists." The surest way to botch a leadership transition and lock people into the past is to send the message that they cannot talk about the previous leader. Again, in Blanchard's words, this is an obstacle posed by the ego—and ego means Edging God Out.

An example that pastors could learn from comes from a choir director in a large church who described how her ministry began. When Leta realized she was following a popular and effective predecessor named Martha, she called her on the phone. This began regular communication. Whenever she had a conversation with Martha, Leta would share with the choir that she had talked with Martha and would convey Martha's greeting to the choir. When Martha came to town, Leta would invite her to sing in the choir. When Leta was visiting in another city where Martha was the choir director, Leta was introduced to the congregation and invited to direct the choir.

As a result, members of the church were at ease with their past leader and their present one. They did not have to be anxious that conversation about their past leader would create a conflict with their new one, or vice versa. They were not placed in a position of making choices regarding loyalty. This was extremely effective as a transition strategy. Leta described this experience as uncommon among choir directors; however, it seems to follow the model of Jesus.

Finally, members need to have the leader *confirm* the importance of the past. As we develop, we generally are trying to find integrity in our lives. It is important to discover that a common thread has been running through our years, and that life is not merely a series of events that have no relationship to one another. Members and leaders need to confirm that past experiences, including those with a predecessor, made an important contribution to the drama of their lives even when a significant change has to be made. Taken together, talking, listening, and confirming help fulfill the spiritual principle introduced by Jesus: Honor thy predecessor.

Principle Two: Build on Health

Jesus said, "Therefore every teacher of the law who has been instructed about the kingdom of heaven is like the owner of a house who brings out of his storeroom new treasures as well as old" (Matthew 13:52 NIV).

Jesus reached into the treasure chest of the past and pulled out what was healthy and strong, thus fashioning the timbers of the new work He was building. Many of the stories Jesus told were not original to Him; neither were many of His ideas. Jesus knew where to find islands of health in His tradition, and that is where He planted His feet.

Jesus knew that the history of His people held pockets of disease and dysfunction. What we now call the Old Testament spoke of polygamy and concubines. Some Scripture seemed to permit a system of divorce that left women impoverished. Jesus did not allow Himself to get lost in an ocean of dysfunctional thinking and debate from the past. He went straight to the Scriptures that spoke about health in marriage—that a man should leave his father and mother, cleave unto his wife, and the two become one. Knowing that some Old Testament laws were less helpful than others, Jesus zeroed in on the greatest commandment, the one most visionary and grounded in health: "Love the Lord your God with all your heart, soul, strength, and mind" (Deuteronomy 6:5 NIV).

Today, one prevailing stream of thinking about leadership transitions tends to be *illness-based*. A pastoral departure is treated like a terminal diagnosis; just as no one plans for cancer, no one plans for a leadership transition either. Once the leader has moved, grief sets in. Organic change has taken place. A death has taken place. The congregation is wounded in all the ways an individual is wounded by a personal loss, and it responds in a similar pattern. Denial, anger, depression, guilt, bargaining, and finally acceptance are the stages of grief played out in the congregation as the members experience loss. An entire body of literature has grown up around this illness-based approach to leadership transition.

At the same time, the grieving congregation also experiences organizational change, which is the inevitable companion to leadership change. It is in the process of moving from something to something. At first, the congregation externally experiences denial, then moves it internally to resistance, and then on to exploration of what these changes will be and how they affect the individuals involved. Finally, external commitment completes the cycle. Some people move through the steps of organic or emotional change and organizational change rather quickly; for others it is so painful they never completely recover. Unfortunately, some congregations are allowed (sometimes encouraged) to focus on their wounds and weaknesses rather than the islands of health that could be a source of strength and renewal. Further discussion about health-based transition in contrast to illness-based transition can be found in Chapter Three.

It is sad to admit that many consultants, interim pastors, and denominational agencies have a vested interest in the illness-based model of leader transition. Reinforcing the weaknesses of a congregation and focusing on wounds makes the congregation more dependent on the "healer." Sometimes, it creates an opportunity to chasten a maverick congregation, bring it back into the fold, and make the members "healthy" again. It is also a way to excuse poor performance just as we excuse sick people from having to go to work. The question Jesus put to the man by the pool is often relevant to a church in transition that is illness-focused: "Do you want to get well?" (John 5:6 NIV).

Considerable pressure is often brought to bear on a new leader to fix what is broken. Get inactive members to come back. Restore the women's association to its former strength. Visit unhappy members. Listen to stories about problems with the former leader. Yes, tend to wounds, but don't focus entirely on grief. Focusing on these pockets of dysfunction is a poor transitional strategy. Jesus knew that. Build on health.

Principle Three: Complete the Past

Jesus was a master at completing the past. The past was neither His whipping post nor His prison. The past was the first stage of a two-stage rocket headed upward.

Jesus understood John the Baptist's role as preparatory to His work; there was no arrogance here relative to John. Jesus understood His own work as preparatory to that of His disciples; He understood the past as the forerunner of the present. Just as the tree carries its history in its rings, the present carries the past and gives it a new surface. Jesus indicated that He did not come to abolish the law, but to fulfill it. Every student of the Bible knows that when Jesus speaks about fulfilling the Old Testament, He does not mean "make it come true." When Jesus fulfills the Old Testament, He completes it by giving it new meaning. Through Jesus, we understand that the complete and full meaning of a promised land is not a piece of geography, but an eternal life.

The default succession plan for kings in the Old Testament is frequently assassination. "Zimri came in, struck him down and killed him in the twenty-seventh year of Asa, king of Judah. Then he succeeded him as king. As soon as he began to reign and was seated on the throne, he killed off Baasha's whole family. He did not spare a single male, whether relative or friend. So Zimri destroyed the whole family of Baasha . . ." (I Kings 16:10–12 NIV).

Another example: "As soon as Baasha began to reign, he killed Jeroboam's whole family. He did not leave Jeroboam anyone that breathed, but destroyed them all . . ." (I Kings 15:29 NIV).

Not only was the previous king killed, but the fruit of that king's life—children and accomplishments—was also destroyed. This is one approach to the past: try to obliterate it. Here, we must reflect soberly. The operation of the human ego in pastors can work against a healthy pastoral transition. The ego does not want to "adopt" the effective ministries that were the "children" of the previous pastor; it wants to have its own children. There is nothing wrong with the drive to be a creative presence in the congregation one is serving, to go beyond repeating the past. It is best to think of a pastoral transition as a blended family in which former effective ministries are adopted by the new pastor while new ministries are birthed as well.

Jesus did not deal with the past by assassination, but by completion. He generally assumed that the past was the necessary path to the present. The role of the new leader is to discover how he or she can complete the work of a previous leader or take it to a higher level.

Many older pastors have a tradition of superb pastoral care and visitation. Upon their retirement, it is likely that the new pastor is younger and has a philosophy of pastoral care espousing more lay involvement and equipping. The tendency is for the pastor to engage certain members of the church in a debate about whether a pastor should be doing all the pastoral care or not. This creates a win-lose situation relative to the past. However, it is possible to see the excellent pastoral care provided by the previous pastor as the necessary stage in developing a more widely shared (and often more effective) member care ministry. This approach sees the work of the previous pastor as setting the standard for excellence to be followed by a capacity building and maturing within the congregation that meets those high standards and expands the ministry to more people. Under the creative impetus of the Holy Spirit, it is always possible to frame one's work as completing the good work of another. That's what Jesus did.

So we see three Biblical principles from the life of Jesus relating to start-up for a new leader: honor thy predecessor, build on health, and complete the past. These are not merely advisory steps for the new leader to consider. They are three principles that church leaders and boards should build into a transition plan as an act of obedience to the Gospel. Any church seeking excellence in a leader transition should use these criteria to screen new leaders, train new leaders, and plan how the transition will be designed and implemented.

Three years later in the life of Jesus, He has a different set of transition issues. He must manage His departure and the succession plan that ensures the continuation of His work. Again, we do not find a detailed succession plan that fits the great variety of church polities, but there are *important wind-down principles*.

Principle Four: Envision Abundance

Jesus refuses to envision scarcity upon His departure. He refuses to envision stagnation in the future of His disciples: "I tell you the truth, anyone who has faith in me will do what I have been doing. He will do even greater things than these, because I am going to the Father" (John 14:12 NIV). The task of forming and articulating a positive vision for the future does not end with a pension for the leader. A leader following Jesus is called to articulate a vision for how the Body can thrive in and through a leadership transition. Anything less is a failure of discipleship.

Faith begins with imagination. The first step toward faith that the mountain will be moved is the capacity to imagine the mountain moving. The leader must be able to imagine a way to unfold a leadership transition that increases maturity, deepens capacity, and fosters abundance rather than scarcity. However, imagination is not enough. God's people may perish for a lack of vision, but they grow cynical when a vision has no substance. As Ron Rand put it, "Works without faith is a body without a spirit. That's a corpse. But faith without works is a spirit without a body. That's a ghost."

The closer Jesus moved to His transition out of leadership, the more detailed He became about what would happen next. He gave clear direction: go into the village. Find a man. Bring his donkey. Go into the village. Find a man. He has an upper room. Prepare a meal. Meet me in Galilee. Wait in Jerusalem. A leader who envisions abundance for the future had better have a specific plan in mind for how the vision will be realized. Every strategic plan should have a strategic target that lays out a transition strategy. The transition plan should have a clear set of actions, with accountability, time lines, and a budget. Envision abundance.

Principle Five: Create Capacity

When a leader moves on, a hole is left in the operation. The hole has two components. The first consists of those irreplaceable qualities that are unique to the leader and impossible to replicate. The second consists of transferable skills that were not transferred. Jesus as Messiah was unique and irreplaceable. Jesus as mentor, teacher, preacher, and healer was replicable. The process of moving expertise from leader to people is called creating capacity, or reproducible ministry.

Jesus began managing His exit transition on the day, and in the way in which, He called His disciples. In Mark 3:14 (NIV), the text says that Jesus appointed twelve. Actually, the word *appointed* in the Greek means "to create." From the beginning, Jesus was creating capacity in the lives of those He called so that they could replicate His work. Notice also that Jesus used the Hebrew method of education, which was not to lecture but to show. Jesus called the disciples to be with Him. He did not call them to attend "fishers of men" classes. He called them to become fishers of men by "talking with them when you sit at home and when you walk along the road, when you lie down and when you get up" (Deuteronomy 6:7 NIV).

Our experience with pastors is that they are comfortable creating capacity at the operational level. Having an office staff with well-managed volunteers and an able volunteer coordinator who never comes in with a problem is a pastor's dream. Having a children's education program that never needs the pastor's help recruiting teachers is utopia. But many pastors are not comfortable creating capacity at the leadership level. They find it threatening to reproduce or transfer what they know to other leaders, or to use the gifts of others that are executive in nature. The reality that many pastors may not want to face is that several of their church members probably have the gifts to lead the church *administratively* as well as or better than they do. Pastors may let laypeople sit in Congress (the boardroom), but they don't necessarily want them in the White House (the senior staff meeting).

A congregation planning for transition needs to build capacity at the leadership level. It needs strategic thinkers and planners. It needs marketing and communication experts. It needs people with skills in personnel recruitment, management, and coaching. It needs people who understand fundraising and financial management. It needs psychologists and counselors who can help high-level people work together in periods of stress without getting entangled in personal issues and baggage. It needs professional artists who can paint and sculpt and sing people into new places. All these people need to be spiritually grounded.

Unfortunately, these are often some of the most underused people in the church. If they were honest, many leaders would admit being afraid to let people with these gifts too close to the reins of power, because they are threatened by such competence. At the same time, some of the most highly skilled laypeople in the workplace become less than adequate in the church because they have not been empowered to use their gifts to the maximum. As a result, a church that is rich in operational capacity has almost no bench strength at the leadership level. When a key leader departs, the church can't field a team. It is important at every level, but especially at the leadership level. Build capacity.

Principle Six: Fight the Demons

By "fight the demons," we are not speaking about exorcism. We are speaking about managing the shadow side of our lives, which tends to emerge with particular strength during times of transition. All in all, we do not see many struggles in the life of Jesus, except around His transitions in and out of leadership. At the beginning, the transition from being a carpenter to an itinerate preacher and healer drives Him into the wilderness. At the end, the transition out of leadership and to the cross drives Him to Gethsemane. There are demons appearing at these points of transition that threaten to scuttle the future.

It is not necessary to go into a lengthy analysis of the spiritual struggles that emerge during a time of significant change. The issues tend to focus on matters of personal identity, worth, and place. Others have dealt with these issues in depth; you should make use of the fine resources readily available.

However, it is important to make the point that struggle around leader transition is almost all emotional and/or spiritual. We are afraid of the topic and therefore do not talk about it. We do not talk about it, and therefore we are afraid of it. The fact that we avoid such issues, make discussion of them taboo, reward silence, punish honesty, and put systems in place that perpetuate dysfunction is a spiritual issue.

Leaders on both sides of the board table must face the unhealthy part of themselves that threatens a successful pastoral transition. Again, secular business may be ahead of the church on this issue. Management texts are now appearing that urge leaders to become aware of their shadow side and make that side visible to others they are leading. Although we would like to assume that a strong Christian commitment obviates a shadow side to the Christian leader, all the evidence shows it does not. When we talk with people about a different approach to pastoral transition, they often give a list of reasons why a different approach is not viable—nearly all of which are emotional rather than theological or practical. On the pastoral side, they include the need to be indispensable and irreplaceable, the need to be totally unique and original, and the need to be in control. On the lay leadership side, demons may appear as the need to be dependent and escape responsibility, or the need to stay in a relatively small personal comfort zone. Conversely, some lay leaders have a need to be in control, to know everything about everything and maneuver themselves into a position of power, filling a vacuum left by a pastor. All of these are emotional and spiritual issues.

There is a final element that belongs here. We call it *recognizing, acknowledging, and containing dysfunction*. Every organization has dysfunctional elements; they tend to emerge as a strong leader begins to recede. We find this happening in the succession work of Jesus. It is at the point of his departure that Judas betrays Him and Peter denies Him. Rather than seeing this as an odd set of events unique to the Son of God, we should see this as the expected emergence of the dysfunctional side of an organization at a time of leadership transition.

We find a further example of this in the early Church. Listen to the words of Paul as he prepares to leave the church at Ephesus in the hands of local leaders: "I know that after I leave, savage wolves will come in among you and will not spare the flock . . . so be on your guard!" (Acts 20:29, 31 NIV). In a healthy church, the leader holds back the emergence of dysfunction by his or her mere presence. This is a ministry invisible to all but a very few. When the leader departs, these elements tend to emerge.

A health-based approach to pastoral transition does not deny the dysfunctional elements present in the organization. However, it refuses to focus its energy on fixing those elements as its primary transition function. It is important for the leader to have some thoughtful strategy for containing this dysfunction. The spiritual work of staying centered and focused while holding off negative forces that threaten to harm the church requires faith, humility, and wisdom. There are both spiritual dimensions and process dimensions of this task. To deal with them effectively, we need to fight the demons in ourselves (not in others) and establish good processes that do not allow dysfunctional elements to undermine what is healthy. As churches follow Jesus in the transition process, each has its own wilderness and Gethsemane. But there comes the promise that each will also have its own "return in the power of the Spirit" and "resurrection into new life."

These transitional principles should be woven into the leadership culture of a church. Since all cultural changes begin with senior leadership, the sea change we are describing must begin with the teaching, coaching, and modeling of the senior pastor. But these principles should be observed for any staff transition— music director, youth leader, program director, education director, administrative staff. The starting point is the interview process, when questions should be posed to the candidate related to his or her history of starting up and winding down in previous positions, plans for managing the transition in and out of the position applied for, and the person's level of openness to transition training.

The checklist in Exhibit 1.1 helps you measure your ability to work through times of transition.

Exhibit 1.1.

Pastoral Transition Principles

Start-Up Principles

When reflecting on my start up, members would say that:

- ☐ I spoke the name of my predecessor to members of the church in a way that was natural and comfortable.
- ☐ I listened to members talk positively about the contributions of my predecessor, without appearing threatened.
- ☐ I confirmed to them the importance of what my predecessor had contributed to the church.
- ☐ I focused on what was healthy and strong from the church's past.
- ☐ I built upon ministries from the church's past that were solid, and I took them to a new level.

Wind-Down Principles

When reflecting on my wind-down, members would say that:

- ☐ I have given the church a vision of strength and abundance beyond my tenure as pastor.
- ☐ I have brought leadership to the church in developing a pastoral transition plan.
- ☐ I have worked to create capacity in the church that will help carry people through the pastoral transition.
- ☐ I have taught and coached wind-down principles with my staff.

Managing the Shadows

When reflecting on managing the shadows, members would say that:

- ☐ I am aware of my shadow side and how it would sabotage a good transition process.
- ☐ I have shared my transitional shadows appropriately with other staff members and lay leaders.
- ☐ I have taught and coached lay leaders to deal with their transitional shadows.
- ☐ I have taught and coached my staff to deal with their transitional shadows.

Chapter Two

Counting the Cost

If today you will be a servant to these people and
serve them and give them a favorable answer, they
will always be your servants.

—*I Kings 12:7 (NIV)*

Solomon reigned in Jerusalem over all Israel forty
years. Then he rested with his fathers and was buried
in the city of David his father. And Rehoboam his
son succeeded him as king. . . . King Rehoboam
sent out Adoniram, who was in charge of forced
labor, but all Israel stoned him to death. King
Rehoboam, however, managed to get into his
chariot and escape to Jerusalem. So Israel has been
in rebellion against the house of David to this day.

—*I Kings 11:42, 12:19 (NIV)*

As Rehoboam learned, a botched succession can be costly. In his
case, the failure to recognize that he did not instantly carry the
authority of his predecessor and could not impose his leadership by
fiat cost him a rebellion that would forever weaken the tribal alliance.
Conquest, deportation, and poverty were the result. What
Rehoboam did was change the contract between his government and
his people. As we describe in Chapter Four, these contracts are constructs in organizational culture, and a sudden change can be costly.

"Nothing educates like an invoice." Those wise words came
from the young chair of a church finance committee. If the model

of Jesus is not enough to educate us toward better leadership transition, then perhaps an invoice is. Our current way of carrying out change in leadership is not only questionable from a Biblical perspective; it is also extremely expensive. Let's dive into the teeth of it. Let's talk about money.

Review the Invoice

It is accepted as an industry standard that the cost of replacing a professional is roughly equivalent to the annual salary of the position. The cost of replacing a pastor is even higher. Let's take a mainline denomination as an example. Assume a church with a worship attendance of 750 persons; a budget of a million dollars or more; and a compensation package for the pastor, including benefits, of $150,000. The common thought that a church will save money on the departing pastor's compensation package during an interim time is simply not true. Generally, all things considered, a full-time interim pastor requires and receives a higher compensation package for the interim. Though the salary may be less, the cost of relocating the interim pastor and furnishing temporary housing raises the package significantly. In addition, there are travel costs involved to maintain family connections.

On the basis of our experience, we estimate that worship attendance typically drops about 15 percent when an effective pastor leaves, since resident associate pastors or an interim pastor are rarely as strong in leading worship as the pastor who has just departed from the church. A church of 750 worshippers will drop in attendance to approximately 635 each Sunday. With the exception of printing, worship costs are generally fixed, so savings that accrue to a smaller attendance are minimal. However, the level of giving generally tracks worship attendance. A drop in giving may lag slightly as people temporarily send in their offering without attending. The church loses financial support of 15 percent or so on a million-dollar budget—approximately $150,000 a year, or about $200,000 in the eighteen months it takes to find a new pastor.

Once a new pastor arrives, giving does not immediately rebound and may take six months to return to its previous level. This calculates to a further loss of about $33,000. This puts the two-year income loss at about $233,000.

Then there are the costs of recruitment. Assume that the search committee consists of nine people. The direct cost of the recruitment effort has to cover printing, postage, travel, moving expenses, temporary lodging, and meals. A typical search committee budget might be $30,000. Add this cost to the revenue loss, and the new total loss is $263,000.

It is likely that the compensation package for the new pastor will be 10 percent higher than for the previous pastor. This additional $15,000 expense for the first year pushes the total to $278,000. Without counting the equivalent cost of the volunteer labor that has been diverted from other forms of ministry to the search process, the financial cost of a pastoral transition in a large church exceeds *twice* the annual compensation package, or 10–15 percent of the annual operating budget of the church. That's money!

Other circumstances can make poor timing on a pastoral transition a financial trauma for the church. If the transition occurs during a major debt retirement process, a shortfall in revenue can be detrimental to programs since debt payments are a fixed cost that are difficult to quickly renegotiate. Short-term cuts in program are the likely fix. If the transition occurs just prior to a major debt reduction campaign, the proceeds are likely to suffer since any successful financial campaign is usually dependent on the confidence provided by the presence and strong support of the pastor.

Beyond the Dollar Cost

There are other costs—emotional and organic costs. The organizational cost and the emotional/and organic costs are now on a collision course. The departure of the leader is one thing, but now the trickle-down effect takes its toll. The collateral impact on other staff members can be substantial. It is not unusual in a large church for the new pastor to want to select his or her own team. Staff members know this. Rather than waiting to see what the new pastor will do, staff members may take the decision into their own hands and find positions in other churches. Even though pastoral staff members may have the technical security provided by polity, the reality is that an associate pastor who does not click with the senior pastor will not be able to stay. (The time and expense of searching for and bringing new staff becomes a considerable expense when one considers the length of time on the learning curve to get up to speed at the church. This could easily be another $50,000.) Again, the taboo against honest discussion of these issues may result in a series of surprise resignations that the governing board has no power to stem. The loss of effective staff members leaves program holes that the board is reluctant to fill until the new pastor arrives. This erodes discipleship, fellowship, and outreach ministries. These losses further affect worship attendance and financial giving, but more significantly they may have an impact on the pool of future leaders in the church. It is not unusual for a church that goes through a poor transition in the first year to have trouble recruiting leaders in the second year.

The costs mount further for the lay leaders of the church. Because no transition plan is in place, lay leaders have to create a plan at the same time they are implementing it *and* trying to manage the general issues of church board work. They can find themselves managing a cascade of issues on a crisis basis, which raises the risk of bad decisions. Attention is diverted from strategic thinking that is essential in such a transition to managing crises. Islands of health in the church are ignored as energy is diverted to putting out fires. Drops in revenue (discussed earlier) force reprioritization of budget items, a process that can further drain energy. The tyranny of the urgent consumes the precious time of leaders who ought to be involved with planning the work of transition and working that plan.

Then there is the morale cost. All these issues potentially affect morale. But our research tells us something else. Morale in a church goes up and down with the quality of a pastor's worship leadership. Our experience tells us that when interim pastor worship leadership is generally not strong, morale drops further.

Undoubtedly, someone will object that these challenges become opportunities for the church to experience a renewal of faith and dependence on God. From that line of reasoning, it would follow that people should spend themselves into debt in order to become more dependent upon God. That's just lousy stewardship. If we are going to place ourselves in a position of dependence upon God, let's find ways of expanding the kingdom of God as opportunities for spiritual renewal rather than contraction and chaos.

In time, a new pastor arrives on the scene and finds himself or herself on the steep slope of a huge learning curve. Because systems may discourage contact between the pastor and a predecessor, critical pieces of information are not shared—the equivalent of traveling around a large city without a map. Veteran leaders know that land mines abound in any church. Without a map, some of them will be exploded. Without a map, new leaders do not know the location of wells (people who are sources of refreshment), food (people who feed the soul), banks (people who have critical resources), fire hydrants (people who can help you put out fires), schools (people who have important information for you), priests (people who will keep confidence), grapeviners (people who broadcast information), and museums (people who have the history). A person can learn the way around a large city without a map, but it takes a long time. That's a cost!

There will be many wrong turns, and failed expectations. In fact, about half of the members of the search committee (and sometimes all of them) leave the church within three years of the new pastor's arrival. That's a cost!

If the transition is handled poorly, the new pastor may become an unintentional interim and stay only a few years, and the whole search process and expense occurs again. That's a cost!

If the previous pastor retires and stays in the community without a clearly defined role and a way to be useful in the church, a division may occur between members with conflicting loyalties. That's a cost!

If the previous pastor retires and stays in the community without a clearly defined role and a way to be useful to the church, a valuable resource may be sidelined in order to protect the new pastor's ego. That's a cost!

So, this is the invoice, or the bottom line. It is only an estimate of what can happen if the traditional model of leadership transition is followed. Clearly, the costs can be considerably different if there is sufficient advance planning for transition. Unfortunately, those who are trapped by what has always been will end up forking over the price of this invoice.

Good Intentions, Costly Results

Consider this composite illustration of several churches. Candlewick Community Church was a vibrant suburban congregation with two worship services and about a thousand people in attendance. In the early 1980s, the pastor developed a unique approach to discipleship that combined spiritual discipline and physical health. The program quickly became national in scope, with extensive speaking and conference leadership responsibilities for the pastor. With the burgeoning program came the need for additional facilities, and so the church embarked on a multi-million-dollar renovation and addition.

Within two years of completion of the building, the pastor suddenly left for another call. Because the pastor had been instrumental in its vision and development, he took the discipleship program to his new church. In following this course, the pastor was adopting standard transitional procedures of creating a firewall between his tenure as pastor and that of his successor. The denominational policies of his church discouraged any bridging strategies that might have lent continuity between his ministry and what followed. He also knew that the church was in no position to carry forward the specialized ministry that he had begun there and that now had a national market. His decision to take the ministry with him was carefully and prayerfully weighed.

Members at Candlewick were conflicted about this. On the one hand, they knew they had no capacity to keep the ministry going, let alone continue its growth. On the other hand, they felt totally unprepared to deal with all the issues left for them. At the very moment they needed to pull together, the church was divided, with no plan to move forward. Some management specialists argue that 85 percent of all employee failures are attributable to deficiencies in the system. In this case, the system worked against both the pastor and the church.

The lack of a clear bridging strategy created pain and frustration among members who now felt simultaneously saddled with a capital debt and the loss of a revenue source. A negative spiritual and emotional climate led to a hemorrhage in attendance that cascaded into a revenue loss. The predictable emphasis on stewardship at a time when surveys were showing that the number one reason people did not go to mainline churches was an overemphasis on money led to further losses that were not recouped by new members. The church ended up in the whirlpool of needing more money in the short run but finding that talking about the need for money was jeopardizing the long run.

In an effort to staunch the losses and turn the church around, members called a pastor steeped in church growth strategies. This was an abrupt change of course. Church growth strategies did not necessarily meld well with the family culture created by the predecessor, and even though the new choice of a pastor made sense strategically, it created a culture clash within the congregation that precipitated further losses.

In the five years encompassing the departure of the pastor and the first three years of the new pastor, worship attendance dropped from a thousand to fewer than two hundred, as parishioners went to other churches or dropped out of the church scene in disillusionment. Revenue dropped from nearly $1 million to less than $200,000. Attendance and revenue numbers plateaued at these levels for ten years, for a total financial loss on the order of $8 million. Other less tangible qualities such as morale, spiritual vitality, community impact, ecclesiastical leadership, and fellowship were concomitant to the financial losses.

It is important to note that in this illustration everyone followed the rules of the current transitional paradigm—the departing pastor, the church board, the regional governing body, and the arriving pastor. Unfortunately, the current church paradigm is a disaster for large churches that think of themselves as a close church family with some significant and unique ministries that are theirs alone. Standard procedures tend to mishandle or ignore these unique mission components (see Chapter Ten), which may have become central to the church's ministry. Nor do they adequately attend to cultural issues within the congregation that may sabotage appropriate strategic objectives, and they do not foster an environment in which bridging structures can be constructed prior to the pastor's departure. The difficulties that might have been created by constructing a transition plan five years before the pastor's departure pale in comparison to the multiple crises experienced by a church bound by taboo.

Staff Retention Plan

Because *all* staff transitions are costly, the first priority for a church that has a high-quality, high-performing staff is a staff retention plan. This is especially important given the current shortage of leadership in the church (and in society at large). Like other organizations, churches are in a highly competitive environment for talent. Keeping the good leadership you have is the first priority of a strategic plan encompassing staffing. There are seven components to a good staff retention plan:

1. A set of clear expectations defining what it means for the staff member to be successful. Without this clarity, staff members

do not know if and when they have hit a home run. Or they are subject to the capricious judgments of a committee or other staff members, which vary day by day depending on who is speaking.

2. A candid discussion regarding the staff member's career goals and needs in a working environment. A good evaluation process evaluates not only the employee but also the way the system is enhancing or hindering full performance. No system can meet all the needs of a staff member, but it can leverage resources to optimize performance, development, and satisfaction.

3. A reliable, functionally appropriate, and discriminating evaluation instrument. Some version of a 360-degree evaluation instrument, which collects data from direct reports, supervisors, and cohorts, requires a significant time investment but can be effective in giving the staff member a good multidimensional measure of his or her performance.

4. A quality coaching and training program. The staff member should have an opportunity to specify what is needed to be successful, and the wise church will offer task-appropriate training and coaching that meets mutually agreed specifications.

5. A competitive compensation package. The package should be benchmarked against regional standards for the position and reflect the performance quality of the individual. Replacement costs, which are generally high (the message of this chapter), should also be kept in mind when setting compensation level.

6. A clear commitment from the church regarding the staff position. In a pastoral transition, what will the board do? Will the trustees ask for letters of resignation from every member to be handed to the new pastor (to be activated or destroyed)? Will the board members guarantee several years of tenure? Will they provide a severance package?

7. A willingness to re-recruit high-quality staff members at a critical juncture. As we mentioned earlier, the cost of recruiting a new staff member is substantial. The board might consider a fraction of that effort in re-recruiting a good staff member as a worthy investment.

Since staff transitions are inevitable at all levels, the church needs a good transition plan at all levels as well. Obviously the most critical transition need is a succession plan delineating a transition in the pastoral position. Generating the motivation to address these issues often requires a dry-eyed local assessment of the costs of a poorly planned and therefore poorly implemented transition process. A worksheet to help with this is at the end of this chapter.

The Big Picture of Long-Term Cost to the Church

Before we leave the subject of cost, it is important to be more global in our thinking, at least for a paragraph or two. As was already mentioned, the leadership crisis in the church is not merely local; it is national. By focusing only on the leadership needs of local churches, we are sowing seeds to rocky soil. We may solve our immediate leadership problem and produce a ministry that flourishes for a short time, but without the roots of transitional thinking and more global leadership bench strength in the church, no enduring fruit will be produced. The failure of churches to call forth, train, and deploy leaders to the larger church community is costly as well, yielding:

- A shortage of both executive and programmatic leadership, which decreases the quality of ministry
- Long recruitment time for new staff members, which leaves quality ministries to drift without effective leadership
- Fatigued search committees that become careless in making background checks and ensuring a good match between candidates and job requirements
- A lack of trained lay leaders who can partner effectively with church leaders at such executive-level functions as strategic planning, marketing, staff development, fundraising, fund management, and facility development

It would be an appropriate mission for larger churches today to develop high-quality, high-level leadership, not merely for themselves but for other churches beyond their own community. This gift, made to the larger church, would make transition planning in other communities more effective. It would be a mistake to envision this task primarily as one to get more people into seminary. Our experience and research tells us that seminaries, though effective at offering academic and theological rigor, are not generally equipped to develop leadership for local congregations.

Having established the spiritual and pragmatic case for a different way of thinking about leadership transitions in the church, we are now prepared to move on to a more practical consideration of how transitions can be accomplished, who the key players are, and the roles they need to play. Exhibit 2.1 was developed from our experience in working with churches to help them forecast the cost of transition.

Exhibit 2.1.

If Your Pastor Were to Leave in Six Weeks and It Would Take Eighteen Months to Find a New One

What Would It Cost?

_____	1. Current average worship attendance
_____	2. Worship attendance in six months (15 percent lower)
_____	3. Current average monthly financial income
_____	4. Average monthly financial income in six months (15 percent lower)
_____	5. Total income lost on an annual basis
_____	6. New members received in the last six months
_____	7. New members received in the next six months (50 percent lower)
_____	8. Search committee costs, 5 percent of general budget, up to $30,000

(Continued)

Exhibit 2.1. Continued.

_____ 9. Increase in compensation package for new pastor (10 percent)

_____ 10. Transition costs for new pastor (housing, movers, transportation, 5 percent of general budget, up to $30,000)

_____ 11. How many other staff members are at risk for resignation whom you want to keep?

_____ 12. Replacement cost for each pastoral or program staff person during transition ($50,000 each)

_____ 13. How many leaders from the search committee will leave the church within three years? (50 percent of members)

_____ 14. On a scale of 1 to 10, with 10 being highest, what is the morale of your church right now?

_____ 15. On a scale of 1 to 10, with 10 being highest, what will be the morale of your church in six months?

Chapter Three

The Five Key Players
in a Healthy Transition

The first task of a winning football team is simply
knowing who should be on the field.
—*Football coach and pastor Don Muncie*

Having looked at the spiritual principles that can guide our thinking on pastoral transitions and at the costs of transitions done
poorly, we now have the necessary motivation to embark on a different journey. We begin this chapter by defining a healthy pastoral transition. Then we move forward by describing how a
health-based model differs from an illness-based model. Finally,
the roles of the key players in a good transition process are defined.

Healthy Transition Defined

A healthy pastoral transition is one that enables a church to
move forward into the next phase of its external and internal
development with a new leader appropriate to those developmental tasks, and with a minimum of spiritual, programmatic,
material, and people losses during the transition. The focus should
be on preserving spiritual, programmatic, material, and people
resources as much as possible during the transition.

Note that this definition is holistic. It does not set spiritual
issues in opposition to material ones. It is difficult for a church to
have a positive spiritual experience when it is bleeding financial
resources every week. Notice also that it is developmental. It
assumes that a church is not a static institution, but a living
organism that is growing and that builds future growth on past

learning. Finally the definition is conserving. In the words of Paul, a healthy transition wants to hold on to what is good.

At a higher level of definition and concreteness, the objectives to be accomplished at the end of a healthy pastoral transition include these:

- *Pastoral recruitment.* A new pastor has been recruited who has the appropriate mix of skills, values, and commitments to match the strategic and internal developmental objectives of the church.

- *Pastoral orientation.* The new pastor has been appropriately oriented to her position through briefings, introductions, mentoring, coaching, information transfers, and record reviews.

- *Communication.* Members indicate that they have been given adequate information through each phase of the transition process, including planning and implementation.

- *Climate indices.* Measures of health in the climate of the congregation around issues of warmth and support, morale, openness to change, conflict management, decision making, and faith centrality have not declined.

- *Financial strength.* Giving, in terms of both total receipts and percentage of household income given to the church, has remained at the pretransition level.

- *Participation levels.* Participation in the life of the church in terms of worship attendance, education, fellowship, and community outreach has remained at the pretransition level.

- *Leadership bench strength.* The leadership reservoir for the church has held steady or increased compared to the pretransition level.

- *Continuity in key ministries.* Key ministries of the church have been sustained across the transition and have the ownership and support of the new pastor.

- *Spiritual strength.* Members understand and have engaged in the spiritual work required to move through the transition, using a clear theological framework and set of spiritual resources made available to them.

- *Role definition of the former pastor.* The former pastor has a clearly defined role in the future of the congregation; it may vary, from mentor or coach to no involvement at all.

Unfortunately, the minutes, documents, and reports of American churches over the last fifty years are littered with accounts of poorly managed leadership transition. Every veteran church leader can recite tales such as these:

- Departing pastors who continue to meddle in the life of the congregation long after their official departure
- Church boards that have no transition plan and become embroiled in the latest crisis du jour during an extended interim
- Regional bodies that exhibit incompetence or a rigid adherence to policies that cling to an outdated paradigm or stifle creativity
- Churches that slowly hemorrhage their vitality and resources, while a volunteer search committee labors over hundreds of resumes and months of interviews
- Newly arriving pastors who are so anxious to establish their own regimes that they plow under an otherwise robust ministry that should be preserved and even showcased

This gallery of failed transitions sits in the collective thinking of church leaders. It leads them to the conclusion that churches in transition become sick.

Illness-Based Transition

Once we accept that churches in leadership transition are sick, grieving, and compromised, a number of corollaries follow.

First, because churches in transition are sick they need time to recover. This requires a long interim, postponement of important decisions, and a slow, laborious search process for a successor.

Second, expectations of sick churches must be lowered. They are not capable of thinking strategically, understanding and implementing best practices, or judging what is worth keeping and eliminating in the church. All these decisions must await the arriving pastor.

Third, sick churches need a doctor and a therapeutic approach to ministry. They are grieving, with all the stages of grief to be observed and articulated. Anger, frustration, depressed morale, and apathy are consistently and systematically assigned to the illness of the church, with encouragement toward catharsis and recovery.

Fourth, sick churches tend to be dependent churches. Some church leaders from denominational churches that were once confident and assertive now become paralyzed with uncertainty as they wade through pages of policies from regional church agencies.

Fifth, sick pastors can't be expected to mentor one another in a transition process or transfer vital information. Their egos are too big and ministry is so arbitrary that arriving pastors can learn little if anything from departing pastors.

This, in a nutshell, is the illness-based model of church transition. No wonder churches avoid the subject as a taboo! Unfortunately, the prophecy is self-fulfilling. The more the subject of leadership transition is avoided, the worse the planning. The worse the planning, the more likely the transition will be traumatic. The more traumatic the transition, the more firmly the illness-based model takes hold in the church at large and the collective consciousness of the religious community.

Health-Based Transition

A health-based model of leadership transition assumes a better possibility. Because it expects that healthy church leaders can actually talk about a pastoral transition without a rash of dependency issues swamping the discussion, it also expects that it is possible to plan for that inevitable day. Since planning for a pastoral transition requires a coordinated effort among several key players, a health-based model assumes that each player is sufficiently healthy and committed to execute a successful transition. A health-based model of pastoral transition also assumes that these players are willing to be equipped with the best practices available for managing one of the most critical seasons in a church's life.

Before moving on to talk about the key players in a health-based transition, it is important to establish what a healthy congregation is. It is difficult to have healthy leaders in a sick congregation. After twenty years of surveying congregations using the Church Planning Questionnaire (see the Appendix to this book), we believe that we have an excellent instrument for assessing overall congregational health. The instrument is completed by a random sample of church members. Then the data are professionally tabulated, analyzed, and compared to a database of information that generates percentile ranks for a number of indices. None of the indices we measure relate to program evaluation. We believe that a church can engage successfully in a number of successful programs (worship, music, mission, youth, and so on) if the general climate of the church is healthy. The list in Exhibit 3.1 presents some salient components of general church health along with the minimum percentage of members who should agree or strongly agree with those assessments in a church that is healthy.

One of the values of this instrument is that it can be used to monitor how the church is doing at various points along the transitional path. If the church is in good general health, it can proceed to plan its transition using a health-based model. If the diagnostic tool discloses problems, then another transitional strategy may be appropriate. See Chapter Twelve for pastoral transition in a low-performance church.

Exhibit 3.1.

___

Indicators of Congregational Health

The congregation is considered to be in good general health if it:

Has vitality in morale (71 percent agreement)
- Members believe they are engaged in meaningful activity.

Has quality fellowship (85 percent agreement)
- Members believe the church fosters an environment that is supportive to members in times of crisis and meets the need for fellowship, friendship, and intimacy.

Embraces change (69 percent agreement)
- Members believe the church is able to embrace change for the sake of more effective ministry to the community it serves.

Manages conflict (70 percent agreement)
- Members believe conflicting points of view are expressed and managed to an optimal outcome.

Has engaged decision making (70 percent agreement)
- Members believe the church engages in a process of leadership selection that is representative and makes decisions fairly and openly.

Sees faith impact (79 percent agreement)
- Members have a high degree of connection between the faith they profess and the faith they practice.

Has vital spirituality (60 percent agree on three times per week or more)
- Members engage in regular and meaningful spiritual discipline.

Enjoys financial generosity (average 2.2 percent)
- Members give a significant percentage of household income to the work of the church; the average household income given exceeds 2 percent.

Has high-performing staff (80 percent agreement)
- Members value the contribution of the pastor(s) and staff to the worship, care, and programmatic dimensions of the congregation's life.

___

Shaping the Team

It is important to identify the key players in a successful leadership transition and define their roles. Our list of key players includes:

The departing pastor
The board
The transition consultant
The personnel committee
The arriving pastor

We have not included the congregation in this list of key players even though the congregation may have the authority to make a final vote on the arriving pastor. Usually the vote is perfunctory and follows the recommendation of the board. A congregation need not become involved in a pastoral transition until the major elements of a plan have been formulated and implemented. A health-based model assumes that church leaders can manage confidential information.

Nor have we included a pastor search committee in the list of key players. A search committee is generally an extension of the board, and we define its role through the role of the board. Sometimes the board may appoint a transition team to manage the transitional tasks for them. We ask you to separate out those functions where a separate search committee or transition team is appointed.

The Role of the Departing Pastor

The role of the departing pastor in a positive pastoral transition has several parts. First, he or she must recognize that every pastor is a departing pastor; the question is not if, but when. This sounds trite, and at the cognitive level it is. Healthy pastors know this at the emotional level as well and are willing to engage the transition issue constructively, without avoidance or manipulation. The planned departure may be in the long run (ten years out or more), in the medium range (five to ten years), in the near term (one to five years), or imminent (resignation announcement is in the mail). An effective pastoral transition at the pastoral level may require two to three years to execute. Ideally, this requires that pastors be in the planning stage several years before they leave.

In addition, not all departures are planned. Pastors are not exempt from maladies that affect other human beings, such as illness, accident, family problems, and sudden death. Unfortunately, some pastors are also fired. These are crisis departures. A healthy pastor wants to make sure that a contingency plan is in place for these scenarios as well. These issues are covered in Chapter Twelve.

Because every pastor is a departing pastor, the day to begin thinking about a transition plan is the day the pastor arrives. This forces the pastor to think strategically, to reflect on what he wants to accomplish in his ministry, and what he wants to offer as a base for his successor to build on.

Second, the departing pastor must participate in developing a transition plan and negotiating how to participate in the execution of that plan. The pastor needs to be clear about how far in advance to announce to the board the intention to leave. Is the pastor willing to overlap his or her successor? Is he or she willing to provide short-term mentoring or information exchange with the successor after departure? Does the pastor need a window of financial security from the church so as to delay the transition into a new position until after the announcement and the beginning of the transition process? The departing pastor must be clear about this with the board.

A word about mentoring is appropriate here. Many pastors are ideally suited to mentor a successor, but others are not. Making a good decision on this issue is critical to a good transition plan. It requires accurate self-knowledge and feedback from others who know the pastor well. Some of the questions a pastor needs to ask himself are listed in Exhibit 3.2.

Exhibit 3.2.

Can You Mentor Your Successor?

Success in the field

- Have I been successful in my work? Does my success continue in the culture in which I am currently serving?
- Is the knowledge I have still relevant to today's environment?

Network of relationships

- Do I have a wide network of relationships and resources with whom I can connect my successor to increase his or her chances of success?
- Positional power

    Am I in a position where I have the power to channel my prestige (pass the mantle) to my successor over time?

Control over resources

- Do I have enough control over resources that I can model how to optimize and manage their use?
- Organizational knowledge

    Do I know how my church organization works?

    Do I have a general knowledge of organizational function and development that I can pass on to my successor?

Track record

- Do I have a good track record in managing subordinates?
- Do I have a good track record in developing teams?

Vulnerability

- Am I emotionally open?
- Am I able to share both the strengths and shadows of my personality?

Intellectual strengths

- Do I have a perceptive mind?
- Am I able to get to the heart of a matter and address the core issues involved?

(Continued)

Exhibit 3.2. Continued.

Storytelling

- Do I have a broad collection of helpful stories and illustrations that I can use effectively in helping concretize abstract principles?

Tailored instruction

- Am I able to tailor instruction to work on issues my successor is addressing now?
- Am I able to foster a process of discovery and exploration rather than one-on-one lecturing?

If a pastor does not believe she can mentor a successor effectively, then she should explore alternative options for transition that offer other sources of training, such as coaching, workshops, coursework, and case studies.

Third, the departing pastor must practice disciplined absence from the board's transition process. The departing pastor frees the board to set a strategic focus for the church, use a church consultant, and choose a successor without interference or manipulation.

Finally, the departing pastor must be willing to keep the promises negotiated as part of the transition plan. This may involve some transitional work with the previous church while beginning work in a new ministry. The pastor understands that the short-term challenge of this period of double service pays dividends in the future effectiveness of the church in which she has made such a substantial investment of her life.

The Role of the Board

The role of the board in a health-based transition revolves around planning and execution. First, the board should have a strategic plan that includes a pastoral transition component. Many boards do not have a functional strategic plan, and those that do rarely give consideration to the most strategic issue the church faces:

pastoral change. By failing to plan for a pastoral transition, the unexpected change can scuttle the best strategic thinking.

Second, the board needs to commit itself to invest the time required to execute the plan. Boards should not expect to abdicate responsibility for this transition by assigning the work to a transition committee or study committee. Even if such a group is appointed, the board must assume major responsibility for the transition elements, of which the transition process is only one. Other major components of a transition plan that require execution are providing specifications for pastoral candidates, updating job descriptions, choosing a transition consultant, identifying unique mission components in the life of the congregation, assessing the maturity and capability of the organization at critical points (see Chapters Ten and Eleven), conducting a final interview, negotiating the final compensation package for the pastor, managing the information transfer from the departing pastor to the arriving pastor, and negotiating any ongoing role for the departing pastor.

Third, the board should select a transition consultant. Since the transition process is so critical to the life of the church, the board must ensure that it has the resources needed to effectively and safely traverse these waters. The board must be free to make its selection without interference from the departing pastor.

The Role of the Transition Consultant

The third key player in a successful transition is the transition consultant. Regardless of the particular polity operating in a church, the time has come for a ministry of professional transition consultants to provide the expertise that is necessary in today's environment. The transition process is too critical to leave to chance or to well-intentioned volunteers who have other full-time responsibilities. The cost of a poorly managed leadership transition justifies the financial outlay required to have a successful one.

Some churches may feel uncomfortable with the idea of using a consultant. It may conjure images of a secular headhunter or placement agency. In reality, consultation services have a long history in the church. In denominational churches, the role of the church consultant has been filled by a regional agency such as a presbytery or a conference. In appointed systems, a bishop fills the role of transition consultant, though one that is narrowly defined as matching candidate to parish. The idea of using specialized expertise during seasons of pastoral transition is not a new one.

The role of the transition consultant is to assist in planning and managing the pastoral transition. First, the transition consultant should be a source of expertise to which a board can turn with utmost confidence regarding pastoral transitions. The consultant should have credentials and experience relative to general strategic planning and be willing to furnish a list of references that can vouch for the quality of work. This is true whether the transition consultant is a paid contractor or a representative of a regional religious agency.

If it appears that the volunteer services extended by a regional agency are not adequate to the task, the church leadership should move to hire a consultant. Hopefully the regional agency and the hired consultant can work cooperatively so that the denominational requirements and strategic requirements of the transition process can be accomplished simultaneously. Again, we assume that in a healthy process the regional agency does not allow rigid adherence to protocol to block an effective transition process.

Second, the transition consultant should be able to assist the board in designing a comprehensive and workable transition plan. This plan should dovetail with the overall strategic plan. It should spell out a specific transition strategy from a menu of options offered by the consultant. It should define in detail the specific role that each key player should fill. It should also spell out the general parameters for negotiating a contract with the arriving pastor.

Third, the transition consultant should assist in executing the transition plan. This includes generating a list of specifications for pastoral candidates, assisting the board in managing the transition issues that arise, and assisting in communication with the congregation and staff.

Fourth, the transition consultant should also serve as the search consultant. In this role, the transition consultant should have access to a pool of potential candidates that can serve as the starting point for the search process. The transition consultant can also do the work of contacting references confidentially, exploring candidate availability and negotiating a final contract.

Fifth, the transition consultant manages the information exchange between the departing and arriving pastors. The consultant brings structure to the exchange that eases any power issues. The consultant also reviews the parameters for both pastors in the transition process as they were established by the board.

The Role of the Personnel Committee

The role of the personnel committee is to set expectations for performance, conduct regular evaluation and coaching, and hold accountability for performance plans. First, the personnel committee should assist the board in developing specifications for pastoral candidates. These should be derived from the strategic plan.

Second, the personnel committee should have a standard evaluation process, including a 360-degree evaluation against annually generated objectives. This process should be fully described to the arriving pastor.

Third, the personnel committee should provide transitional support to the arriving pastor for the first year of ministry. This prevents the premature bonding of the pastor to a few influential members and enables the pastor to keep proper perspective.

The Role of the Arriving Pastor

Finally, we come to the role of the arriving pastor. First, the arriving pastor must be honest with himself regarding the match between his qualifications and the specifications. It is easy for a candidate to become so caught up in the excitement of a new position in a larger church that a sober evaluation cannot occur.

Second, the arriving pastor must be willing to participate in the transitional plan developed by the board. This involves transfer of information through written documents, meetings with other staff members, and structured conversations with the departing pastor. It is important for the arriving pastor to be teachable regarding effective local ministries and the key factors in their success that the pastor must know.

Third, the arriving pastor must be able to publicly honor his or her predecessor without a sense of threat or denial of history. Departing and arriving pastors should have the opportunity to give mutual recognition as a way of minimizing the emotional and spiritual seam at the point of pastoral change.

Transition can take a variety of paths, which you will see in the chapters in Part Two. Regardless of the path, every healthy transition involves these five key players.

Part Two

The Four Church Cultures: Family, Icon, Archival, and Replication

Chapter Four

One Church, Four Variations

When they heard Paul speak to them in their own
language, they became very quiet.

—*Acts 22:2*

A church in the Midwest was doing a mission study in preparation
for calling a new pastor. Unfortunately, the church was rent by conflict. They called us in to do a standard church survey and run a
cross-tabulation. In doing so, we discovered that the group of people who were most unhappy had actually joined the church fifteen
years before that. They were attracted to the church by a free-
spirited pastor who had little patience for the policies of the denomination of which he was a member. When it became clear that the
church was becoming intolerant of their maverick pastor, he left.
The next pastor the church called was the very opposite of his predecessor. He was straight-laced and by-the-book. This abrupt change
in pastoral styles set up a conflict in the congregation that was still
simmering fifteen years later in this large, Protestant church.

A small Roman Catholic church in the same city had a similar scenario. A priest who was progressive and relaxed in his attitude toward church rules was appointed to the parish. He was
loved in the parish until the day he retired. As a corrective, the
bishop sent a successor who was much more observant of church
standards. The new priest encountered some resistance and was
soon moved on to a larger parish by the bishop. That was only
four years ago. The parish now has a new priest who is greatly
respected, and the church is moving forward under his leadership

with no enduring scars from the abrupt transition between a pro-gressive priest and a more traditional one.

For anyone interested in understanding pastoral transitions, one question cannot be avoided. How is it that a transition in one type of church leaves such deep and abiding scars, while a simi-lar transition in another type of church is remembered as a small bump in the road?

Transition can indeed be viewed as a positive and growing experience. Why do some churches seem more tolerant of pas-toral transition than others?

Understanding Church Cultures

The answer lies in church culture. When the free-spirited Protes-tant pastor held office, he created a culture around his own oper-ational style that was attractive to a large number of people in the early 1970s. Maintaining this culture was part of the unspoken agreement that members entered into as they joined the church. When a new minister arrived with a different operational style, the culture changed abruptly. Members felt that the church they had joined and promised to support was gone.

The culture of a Roman Catholic church is different. An individual priest does have an impact on a parish culture, but the codification and standardization of church life, particularly in worship, tends to prevent wholesale reshaping of the culture around the pastor. In addition, the unspoken agreement that many Roman Catholics enter into when they join a parish is less focused on particulars within the parish than it is upon the uni-versal and less transient aspects of the Roman Catholic Church. The culture is more resilient in the face of pastoral changes because expectations of the members are different.

A significant aspect of church culture is the social contract between a church and its members that keeps them connected. This social contract is the glue that holds a church together. It is an implicit contract; nowhere is it articulated, and many members may not be able to state precisely the agreement they have struck. However, if the contract is violated, they vote with their feet, their pocketbooks, or their negative emotional energy, even if they can't say exactly why.

From the member side, the elements of the contract that they will bring to the church are presence, engagement, resources, and marketing. From the church side, the elements of the contract that the church provides to the members are services, impact, intimacy, and inclusion. The implicit contract for a small church participant might look something like this:

As a member, I will do the following:

- Be present in worship and seasonal activities (presence)
- Be engaged in service as an usher (engagement)
- Provide $1,000 a year and three hours per week of my time (resources)
- Tell people what a wonderful church we have (marketing)

On the condition that the church:

- Provides regular worship services at a time I can attend, and offers routine pastoral care and crisis care when I am sick or in difficulty (services)
- Allows me the opportunity to have my opinion make a difference in the direction of the church; therefore the church will not make radical changes without consulting me (impact)
- Gives me opportunities for knowing people in the church as a family (intimacy)
- Includes me as an insider, rather than tolerating me as an outsider (inclusion)

It is interesting to note that if this contract changes from the church's side, the member will likely change as well, especially if

- The pastor decides to stop doing annual visitations in the home and trains the laity to do so
- The congregation is no longer permitted to vote on the budget

- The congregation becomes so large that the member does not know everyone
- An influx of new people from the community makes the member feel on the outside

Then the member may alter his or her contract with the church by reducing involvement, withholding money, or leaving. It is important to realize that a church in North America can be decimated not by doing anything unethical, unscriptural, or heretical but *merely by changing the implicit social contract held by a majority of members in the church.*

The impact of a pastoral transition upon a congregation is shaped by the church culture and the expectations that members bring to their church experience. Each church culture generates its own expectations. If these expectations are ignored in the transition process with a one-size-fits-all approach, the results can be painful and costly.

American churches are incredibly diverse, and it is unreasonable to list all the variations in the social contract that serve as this congregational glue. However, we can broadly group churches into several categories for the purpose of thinking about leader transition. In this chapter, we think primarily about pastors, though other leaders could be considered as well in the model.

What Drives a Church?

Let's consider what it is that drives a church. At the human level, a driver is the propellant that gives energy to a church. Broadly speaking, churches are driven by either *knowledge* or *personality*. Of course, both knowledge and personality are important to a church. But generally a church chooses one as the primary driver of its corporate life and relegates the other to an auxiliary function. Some churches are personality-driven; others are knowledge-driven.

In the personality-driven church, the pastor uses his or her personality as the primary resource for accomplishing the mission. There is an emphasis on the relationship with the pastor and the benefits of that relationship through pastoral care; influence;

political function; or the unique gifts of the pastor related to presentation, communication, or charismatic function.

In the knowledge-driven church, the pastor uses specialized knowledge as the primary resource for accomplishing the mission. There is an emphasis on the knowledge that the pastor holds regarding history, tradition, and liturgy or to the knowledge that the pastor is skilled at transmitting through teaching, training, coaching, or mentoring. The critical knowledge can be Biblical, theological (a particular theological perspective), practical (how to share faith, how to listen therapeutically), or social (how to work for justice).

Of course, pastors serve in both these roles. Generally, they prefer to function in one role more than another, and the members expect this to be so. The member expectation becomes part of the social contract that glues them to the Body.

In addition to drivers connected to the pastor, there are generally two sets of criteria that members use to judge the success of the church. Broadly speaking, members judge that the church is successful either through *style* criteria or *effectiveness* criteria.

In an effectiveness-based church, the members evaluate its success according to how successful the church is in accomplishing its mission. There is an emphasis on evaluation, benchmarking, and best practices. Many mainline denominations chaff at the concept of "success" as a criterion for their churches. However, even a church as committed to social justice as the Presbyterian Church indicates in its governing documents that the church must be open to changing its institutional forms so that they are faithful *and useful*.

In a style-based church, the members evaluate the success of the church by how well the leadership preserves a certain style or tradition regardless of effectiveness. There is an emphasis on history, tribe, and ritual.

If we combine the two pastoral drivers with the two criteria for success, we can develop a chart with four quadrants that represent church cultures (Exhibit 4.1).

Members in these four church types have differing implicit social contracts that glue them together. In addition, the four church types represent four cultures. Though all have allegiance

Exhibit 4.1.

Four Church Cultures

Personality-Driven Style Church **Family culture** Pastor as parent, elder, brother or sister	*Personality-Driven Effectiveness Church* **Icon culture** Pastor as living logo
Knowledge-Driven Style Church **Archival culture** Pastor as activist curator	*Knowledge-Driven Effectiveness Church* **Replication culture** Pastor as replicator of ministry

to Jesus Christ, they have four distinct sets of ideas governing them, often their own vocabulary, an identifiable set of values, their own set of rewards and punishments. As differing cultures, each church type has its own feel and distinct role for the pastor.

The Four Cultures

A *family culture* expects the pastor to maintain and guide the church as a parental figure who carries the family traditions and heartbeat. An *icon culture* expects the pastor to symbolize in his or her public persona the character of the church and to be the face or voice through which people enter the church. An *archival culture* expects the pastor to be an activist curator. It insists that the pastor be in touch with the great historical and universal traditions of the church so that they can be made relevant to the present. A *replication culture* expects the pastor to replicate ministry through multiplication of called, equipped, and deployed leaders and workers.

None of these church types is "pure." For example, all church cultures have elements of family. However, a family culture is distinct in that the elements of relationship and style drive the decision making of the church and become central to the expectations of members. In addition, no one church type is superior to another. Each has its strengths and vulnerabilities. These church types correspond to the variety of churches found in American society. Examples are found in Exhibit 4.2.

Each of these cultures responds in its own way to a pastoral transition. How a Roman Catholic church (archival culture) deals with a new priest and a departing priest is quite different from how a small Presbyterian church (family culture) deals with a newly called pastor and a departing pastor. It is helpful for churches to understand what they are as they begin to look seriously at how to deal with a pastoral transition.

Exhibit 4.2.

Four Church Cultures, with Examples

Personality-Driven Style Church
 	
Family culture
 	
Pastor as parent, elder, brother or sister
Examples:
    Most mainline Protestant churches
    Smaller community churches
	Personality-Driven Effectiveness Church
	
	Icon culture
	
	Pastor as living logo
	Examples:
	    Media churches
	    Many megachurches
	    Large mainline Protestant churches

Knowledge-Driven Style Church
 	
Archival culture
 	
Pastor as activist curator
Examples:
    Roman Catholic Church
    Orthodox Church
	Knowledge-Driven Effectiveness Church
	
	Replication culture
	
	Pastor as replicator of ministry
	Examples:
	    Some megachurches
	    Parachurch organizations

Exhibit 4.3.

Personality-Driven Style Churches: Family Culture

Family culture is ultimately concerned with maintaining a way of life that has integrity and familiarity. This integrity is often rooted in a set of traditions that gives a sense of continuity with the past and predictability to the future.

The style can take many forms depending upon the church, but what all such churches have in common is a focus on a particular way in which a leader relates to the congregation. This may mean a particular approach to pastoral care, a method of in-home visitation, hospital visitation, or sending notes and cards. It might also include special rituals in worship or special seasonal services to which a pastor adds an idiosyncratic touch.

Over time, the style becomes ritualized into a set of traditions. If the tenure of the pastor is long enough, these traditions can span several generations and become an important expectation in the minds and hearts of the people. Any failure of the tradition in relationship to the leader is experienced as a significant loss to the community and to individuals within it.

In a family culture, results are not as important as the experience of continuity. Measuring effectiveness feels as inappropriate to this church as measuring the effectiveness of a family. Indeed, the group dynamic of a personality-driven style church tends to be that of a family with someone (sometimes a pastor) serving as the parent. The father or mother becomes the significant decision-making power within the church and often holds veto power over more formal decision mechanisms within the church.

The church learns to expect that when the leader is involved almost all experiences will be meaningful. This fosters a level of trust and confidence in the leader. Over time, the leader can be given significant power to make decisions that the governing board will almost always ratify.

Maintaining good personal relationships with the members of the church ensures the long-term success of a leader in a family culture. As time passes and more personal experiences are accumulated, the more profound are the rituals around the leader's work. This produces a deepening sense of community for the members, a greater sense of peace that is based on the dependability of their traditions and their memories of faithfulness.

If a family culture does not develop some commitment to effectiveness, it may yield a congregation of satisfied members yet dwindling in number. In addition, the family dynamic within the congregation fosters a parental dependence. The congregation experiences pastoral transition as a kind of death that often requires a significant period of grief work and recovery before a new leader can be called.

Exhibit 4.4.

Personality-Driven Effectiveness Churches: Icon Culture

An *icon culture* is ultimately concerned with results.

Results may be measured either quantitatively or qualitatively. Quantitative results may measure the number of persons engaged in, attending, or committed to the church as well as facilities, finances, or staff. Qualitative results may include knowledge, task readiness, proficiency, or attitudes. Whether results are quantitative or qualitative, an icon culture focuses on what is being accomplished and how much.

An icon culture capitalizes upon the personality and gifts of a central leader. In large churches, these gifts almost always include an exceptional ability to lead public worship, preach, and teach. There is often a significant television, radio, or tape ministry. The leader may have a distinctive public persona, display a certain flamboyance, or possess a particular stage presence.

Other gifts of the leader may become a focal point for the effectiveness of the church. The leader may have charismatic manifestations related to healing, or an uncanny ability to connect with people who have resources and catalyze their support. Or the leader may be able to envision future possibilities and bring them to fruition.

The church learns to expect that when the leader is involved almost all enterprises are successful. This fosters a level of trust and confidence in the leader that facilitates rapid decision making and resource allocation. The leader is often given broad power to make decisions; governing boards and committees have less frequent meetings than in other churches. More decision-making power may be allocated to the leader and those he chooses for consultation, including trusted staff members or friends.

Because success depends upon the support and engagement of the leader, *icon cultures* often have a top-down management style. This works well because the leader has the level of competence and insight necessary to make good decisions for a range of programs. As time passes and a record of success accumulates, a snowball effect often kicks in. The more successful the leader, the more trusted she is; the more trusted she is, the more successful she becomes.

Given the resources made available to the leader and the leader's ability to gauge what is effective, an icon culture can remain effective over a long pastoral tenure. The continuing vitality and innovative thinking of the leader can ensure future success.

(Continued)

Exhibit 4.4. Continued.

The leader knows that success depends upon a supportive team, a team the leader plays a major role in selecting. However, the team is often not engaged in strategic decision making but is instead expert in operationalizing the vision of the leader. In exchange for their loyalty, the team members are given the resources necessary to provide excellent programming.

If a personality-driven excellence church does not develop enough leadership depth it may find a leadership transition to be extremely painful, expensive, and disruptive. In addition, the success of one central leader may produce a crippling dependence in the long run that hampers efforts for the church to move forward without him or her.

Exhibit 4.5.

Knowledge-Driven Style Churches: Archival Culture

An *archival culture* is ultimately concerned with maintaining a way of life that is grounded in a substantial body of knowledge accumulated over many years. Adherence to this knowledge gives the church a deep connection to its past as well as to churches in other locations that share the same knowledge base. It is common in an archival culture to hear people talk about the benefits of worshiping in other parts of the world and feeling completely at home in a different church that has identical liturgy.

The style can take various forms depending upon the church, but what all have in common is a focus on a particular body of information and a shared commitment to adherence. This information regulates most aspects of church life, particularly its liturgy; the cycle of readings and seasonal emphases; policies relative to sacraments; and standards of entrance, participation, and exclusion. In addition, an archival culture often has clear and universal standards for personal conduct as well as an official position on social issues and international affairs. By their nature, these churches tend to be hierarchical, with a concentration of power at levels above the local congregation that serves to coordinate, regulate, and sustain the tradition.

Although the leaders in this kind of church may have more local authority than those in personality-driven churches, the parameters within which they function are narrower. Since an important goal of an archival culture is to participate in a corporate life that is universal across time and space, there are fewer expectations that the leader will shape the local congregation's ministry into something unique. Homilies in these churches tend to be less a focal point of the corporate worship. Therefore the distinctiveness of the individual homilist, though recognized and even appreciated, does not usually become the basis for participation. The same could be said for such other aspects of church life as governance, policies, and mission. They tend to be more universal for these churches, with fewer opportunities for shaping a church around the perspectives or gifts of a particular leader.

In an archival culture, results are not as important as adherence to the body of knowledge held in the community. Leaders are expected to learn this information in a substantial educational process and maintain a connection to the tradition. Members of this kind of religious community have the comfort of knowing that leaders will come and go but the broad focus and activities of the church do not change. For this reason, leadership transition in these churches is much less traumatic than for the three other types, and this becomes a strength.

However, archival cultures are not without transition issues. Instead of centering on a leader (except at the top), these issues tend to center on changes in the knowledge base. Whereas other church types could be sidetracked by a pastoral transition that took place decades before, archival cultures tend to get stuck on changes in the liturgy, the use of language (for example, Latin versus vernacular), changes in the prayer book, theological or policy changes, and so on.

If a knowledge-driven style church does not shape itself so as to address the culture in which it is living and serving, it risks a cleavage between word and deed. It may exhibit admirable stability but be an undesirable status quo.

Exhibit 4.6.

Knowledge-Driven Effectiveness Churches: Replication Culture

A *replication culture* is ultimately concerned with reproducible results.

As in icon cultures, results may be measured either quantitatively or qualitatively. Quantitative results may measure persons engaged in, attending, or committed to the church as well as facilities, finances, or staff. Qualitative results may include knowledge, task readiness, proficiency, or attitudes. Whether results are quantitative or qualitative, a replication culture focuses upon what is being accomplished and how much.

A replication culture is not necessarily antitraditional in principle as long as traditional approaches are effective. Some churches may even reach back in time and reintroduce archaic practices such as chanting or prayer forms and present them as innovation.

(Continued)

Exhibit 4.6. Continued.

But when an approach or method no longer achieves the desired results, these churches are willing to make significant changes, even if it means giving up long-standing traditions. Worship experiences may be tailored to achieve a particular result even if it means eliminating familiar elements or adding elements that are innovative and controversial. Administrative, programmatic, operational, and mission components may be recast as well, if necessary to ensure effectiveness.

The knowledge that drives this culture is not generally academic or abstract. Above all else, a replication culture is learning how to connect faith with life in concrete and relevant ways. It focuses on best practices in ministry today. Leaders are often well networked with other leaders and connected with sources of information on what is working now.

A replication culture is often aware of the most effective available means of accomplishing objectives. Though usually committed to an orthodox or even fundamentalist approach to Christianity, these churches can make extensive use of knowledge drawn from other fields, particularly marketing, psychology, and adult learning.

A replication culture is often adept at converting information into standardized training materials that enable replication of effective leadership at many levels of the church. Traditional approaches may focus on training church school teachers; replication cultures may provide high-quality training on church management, investment planning, small-group dynamics, personal assessment and integration, leadership, multimedia communication, Biblical interpretation, and so on.

An emphasis on reproducible ministry and excellence gives many of these churches high bench strength. Behind many key leaders stands a cadre of other qualified and committed people. This reduces the risk and cost of leadership transition since the effectiveness of the program is not as dependent upon a particular personality as it is on the body of knowledge possessed by a pool of leaders.

If a replication culture is not careful it may sacrifice principles for results. In addition, if these churches do not develop an adequate relational side, they may have a large back door, with substantial losses of people who have not been able to connect in meaningful relationships. Without the historical experience of an archival culture, a replication culture may end up reinventing the wheel.

Chapter Five

Transition Strategies for Leaders in a Family Culture

> Therefore, as we have opportunity, let us do good
> to all people, especially to those who belong to the
> family of believers.
>
> —*Galatians 6:10 (NIV)*

A *family culture* is driven by the idea that the church assumes the sociological configuration of a family or tribe. Leaders in this culture are not first defined in terms of programs or position but in their particular relationship to the community. There is substantial literature on this culture and the roles that develop within it: patriarch or matriarch, medicine man or medicine woman, tribal chief, and so on. For the purposes of this book, we simplify the model and assume that the primary relationship of the pastor to the culture is that of family member. The pastor is not necessarily a patriarch or matriarch but could be an elder "brother" or "sister." This avoids the implication that members are "children." What is most important is that the core functions are relational rather than administrative and that the pastor is a leader within the family. Though direction is important in many family cultures, the church is not first defined in terms of where it is going. Instead, the church is primarily a place of being and belonging. This means that pastoral transitions may have a significant impact on how members understand their place in the community, which could require significant renegotiation of relationships.

The second idea that drives the family culture is the importance of continuity. Traditions established by the family and its leader are sources of stability and strength in the culture. These traditions take many forms, from who will sing the key song in the annual Christmas program to the pattern of activities in Lent. In any case, these rhythms become a trusted source of stability. The more chaotic the local, regional, national, or global environment, the more important this continuity becomes. Pastoral transitions that interrupt these routines or introduce novel elements can create significant anxiety in a family culture and need to be carefully managed.

A third idea that drives the family culture is the critical role played by boundaries. Family cultures, like biological families, are slow to adopt new members into the fold and may require a significant period of testing for admission. Often there are two separate tracks for admission to the family. The first is the more formal, procedural track required to satisfy the dictates of church polity. This can be accomplished in a relatively short time. The second track is more relational, through which a person is actually "in the family." In larger family cultures, this second "joining" may not occur until a member is initiated into a small group or clan. The final acceptance can take years. Since the process of adopting a new pastor is not significantly different from that of adopting new members, a pastor entering a family culture church can find the community to be exclusive and difficult to enter. The implication for pastoral transition is that completion can require a significant period of time.

Family culture churches tend to have a smaller number of members than those of other church cultures. Because the vast majority of churches in the United States are small, a family culture predominates in the religious environment that most of us have experienced. A larger church can exhibit a family culture if it is formed around a pastor with a strong and largely exclusive tradition of pastoral care. For example, a church with a pastor who does the lion's share of the hospital calling, funerals, weddings, and baptisms, and who has a large pastoral correspondence with members will express many of the characteristics of a family culture. Generally, a growing family culture church crosses a threshold where the pastor can no longer sustain the intimate contact with members. Small-group programs are initiated to further a family feeling in a growing congregation. The pastor becomes a symbol within the community and may begin to use strength of personality to make the church more effective in outreach, evangelism, and community impact. When this happens, the culture is slowly transformed into an icon culture.

Larger, multistaff churches can also exhibit a family culture when the dynamic of the staff is one of "dad" and younger brothers or younger sisters. An alternative family configuration in a multistaff church occurs when each pastoral staff member represents the key family member to one segment of the congregation. Every member belongs to one of the church "families," and every family has a pastor as the key family leader. Because of the range of configurations in family cultures, a number of transitional options need to be considered.

Language in a family culture tends to be shaped around the dynamics of a family unit. The vocabulary includes the expected familial words: brother, sister, spiritual father or mother, godmother, godfather, daughter or son of the church, uncle or aunt (as children may refer to adult members in the church). Groupings of members may be referred to as clans or kinship groups. The church may be called the family of God, the church family, or the gathering of the family. New members are welcomed into *the family*. Family events such as births, birthdays, anniversaries, and reunions receive special attention. Hymnbooks and curriculum may be chosen that have family in the title or a strong familial theme.

The family culture tends to be a feeling culture, which means that decisions tend to be based on personal values and how they affect individuals or groups. Pastors in family cultures tend to be extraverted feelers. This makes them adept at expressing interest in people, warmth, tact, and sympathy, all qualities appreciated by the culture. Transitional planning needs to honor the emotional tenor of this culture by attending to how decisions and actions make people feel. This tends to slow down many processes, since emotions change more slowly than thinking.

The values of a family culture tend to reward shared history, longevity, pedigree, respect, loyalty, local tradition, obedience, insiders, the family unit, children, storytelling, practical service, sacrifice, duty, informality, and being together. The values of a family culture tend to penalize (or are passive toward) an emphasis on effectiveness, discontinuous change, methods, formal processes, experts, credentials, measuring, benchmarking, and outsiders.

Leadership Transition Advantages

There are four leadership transition advantages of a family culture:

1. The culture holds the power to maintain continuity during a time of pastoral transition.

2. Many people in power have a long history in the church. This gives them familiarity with the traditions that are important in the culture.

3. Many people in a family culture have been given informal power. Informal power is a capacity for action outside of formal structures. In a large family culture, the pastor consults with key leaders who may or may not be on the official board in making decisions. The issue is then brought to the board for ratification. In the absence of a pastor, informal leaders can get things done and keep the family running even when there is a significant amount of chaos in the formal leadership structures.

4. Members are accustomed to decisions being made by fiat. Parental figures tend to function autocratically. When important decisions need to be made in a family culture, it can be done even in the absence of a formal leader as long as the informal leaders are in place. Since leadership in these churches tends to be static, members have a sense of stability during pastoral transition.

A family culture church can be deceptively hardy and resilient. Any regional body that has sought to close a small family culture church because of inadequate resources has likely found itself with a tiger by the tail. These churches can be like cacti in the desert, surviving and sometimes thriving in a seemingly impossible environment. Whether small or large, a family culture church can be extremely independent in orientation to the world and require considerable skill in managing pastoral transition.

Risks in Choosing a Candidate

If the pastor in a family culture has become the central leader in a community, the experience of loss can be profound, equivalent to that of a death or divorce. Because the pastor often moves on to another call, one serving a larger community with better remuneration, there may be feelings of rejection along with the loss. This leads to all the classic dynamics of grief that have been well documented: shock, denial, anger, guilt, bargaining, depression, and acceptance.

This grief process leads to several risks for the community in selecting a new pastor. The first is the cloning impulse. Here the church attempts to find a pastor similar enough to the previous pastor to help alleviate feelings of loss. This may lead people to such a focus on certain qualities in a candidate that they overlook other more problematic characteristics. The second risk is the opposite problem, the deficit rebound. If the previous pastor had significant deficits, the church may move in reaction to find a candidate who is the opposite of the previous pastor. For example, the departing pastor might have great pastoral gifts in preaching and caring for people but is less skilled administratively. The search committee desires to address the administrative issues by seeking out a strong administrator, never realizing that it may be sacrificing the pastoral strength that the church has relied on. Again, the focus on certain characteristics may blind the church to other less favorable qualities or move members to select a candidate without taking the whole scope of the relationship into account.

Smaller family cultures may have severely restricted financial resources available to pay a pastor. A small compensation package restricts the potential candidate pool for the church to much-less-experienced pastors or to those near retirement. Younger pastors may not have the savvy required to operate in a family culture where the actual powerbrokers do not necessarily hold office.

Any of these risks can lead a church to select a successor who is less than optimal for the church. The result can be profound disappointment and years of frustration on the part of the pastor and the church. Unfortunately, one may find a family culture extremely painful to deal with in times of disappointment or if one is not granted admission after years of attempts to get in.

Critical Transition Tasks

The two critical transition tasks in a family church are grief management and tradition maintenance. Avoiding the risks in a family culture that we have just outlined above requires a significant engagement in the grief process. Members must have opportunities to mourn their loss. An interim leader with therapeutic skills in grief management can be helpful to a family culture in this time of loss. Members need permission to give expression to their grief in the many and varied ways that people respond to loss. Once members have released a previous pastor and appropriately grieved their loss, they are better equipped to select a candidate who can serve the family in the future.

Tradition maintenance provides continuity in the rituals that are the key to the family culture's well-being. There is an art to determining which local traditions are vital to the community's identity and should not be disrupted and which are tied to the former leader and should be let go. However, this task is critical to the healthy transition in a family culture. If it is mishandled, the congregation will experience two simultaneous losses: they lose effective ministries within their church at the same time they are losing the pastoral relationship. This double loss can be extremely traumatic and in many cases is unnecessary. If care is taken in a thoughtful transition plan to identify key ministries and support them over the transition, a stronger church will await the next pastor.

Threats to Success of the New Pastor

The primary transition threat in a family culture is loyalty conflict. Because a family culture requires that people be loyal to a relationship rather than a set of ideas, members feel conflicted if a successor heads in a direction in which the predecessor would not have gone. The successor pastor is in competition with a person who is present only in the minds of the people. Since this obstacle is not rational, it cannot be dealt with by pointing out the merits of a new idea. It requires the deeper healing of accepting loss.

Other unresolved issues in the relationship with the previous pastor that are generalized to all pastors and played out with the successor are also threats during transition.

The shadow transitional threat in a family culture is a demand for excellence. This is because family cultures tend to value the personal relationship with a leader and devalue the professional competencies that the pastor brings to the task. Family cultures tend to penalize an emphasis on effectiveness and measurement. However, these skills are necessary for any church to survive in the current competitive environment. The denial of this need threatens to become a shadow within the organization that members want to avoid or deny. Family cultures may desperately need this level of competency but not honor it in a successor.

Transition Strategies

There are several transition strategies to be considered for a family culture.

Delayed Arrival

A transition strategy that works well in family cultures is a delayed arrival. This means that there is a delay between the departure of the previous pastor and the selection or arrival of the successor. This gives members an opportunity to work through feelings of loss and emerge into a hopeful attitude for the future. It requires a bridging resource, a leadership asset that the congregation is able to acquire or develop to help carry it across the gap opened up between the departing pastor's leaving and the new pastor's arrival. The function of a bridging resource is to sustain excellence of ministry in the church and assist the church with transitional issues. If the church develops a transition plan well in advance of a pastoral change, it has the time to be creative relative to the variety of possible bridging resources:

- *An interim pastor*—an ordained pastor, often with specialized training related to managing congregations in transition. There are several challenges related to interim pastors. One issue is that the overall shortage of pastors has affected the number of interim pastors. A second issue is timing and availability. A third issue is that many interim pastors have not had experience in larger, more complex churches.
- *Lay professional*—a nonordained professional person, often with formal education and experience in management, marketing, human resources, or a service industry. This background, combined with an authentic spirituality and knowledge of the church as an organism or organization, can make the person a valuable asset during pastoral transition.
- *Skilled volunteer*—a noncompensated staff member who offers his or her services to the church as a contribution. Many middle-aged men and women who have made it in their careers and retired managers and executives are looking for opportunities to make a difference. Given the right authority, opportunities for training, and placement in the organization, they can make important contributions.

Division of Responsibility

A transition strategy that uses several bridging resources in a family culture divides the administrative, pastoral, and worship responsibilities among several persons. This enables the church to function effectively during its search process by finding the best preaching resources available and splitting out the pastoral care or administration functions of lay professionals or volunteers.

Sequential Timing

Another transition strategy that is frequently used in a family culture is sequential timing. Here the new pastor arrives almost immediately after the departure of the previous pastor. Usually this strategy is used in appointed systems with an itinerant ministry, where relationship loss and grief issues are not predominant. There are a number of sequential timing strategies that can be helpful in transition:

- Develop an annual strategic assessment of the church, to include the state of the local church, the state of the community, and clear strategic objectives. This information can guide the local body in its planning and also assist the appointive body in making a good placement.
- Have the local congregational leaders identify "unique mission components" to be shared with the arriving pastor (see Chapter Ten as well as the subsection later in this chapter).
- Conduct a "pastor-to-pastor debrief" after new appointments have been made (see the checklist in Chapter Ten).
- Develop a set of rituals, devotional materials, and transitional activities based on the best research available that can tend to the needs of people relating to loss.

Overlap Timing

Overlap timing creates a period of a week to several months in which both the departing pastor and the new pastor share leadership responsibilities in the church. This overlap period is an opportunity for building relationships between the people and the new pastor, asset transfer (Chapter Ten), mentoring or coaching, and practiced absence on the part of the departing pastor.

One method of implementing an overlap strategy is to create a co-pastor position in the church with equal compensation and authority provided for each position. At the end of the overlap, the co-pastor position is dissolved and the candidate becomes the pastor. Of all the options we have presented, overlap timing is the most emotionally and spiritually demanding. Before this option is chosen, the departing pastor should engage in a period of self-examination and reflection to determine if this is a suitable or realistic option.

Optioned Leadership

Optioned leadership is a strategy that calls a pastor provisionally, to serve for several years (generally two to four) with an option of making the call permanent at the end of that period. With or without overlap timing, this strategy can work well in family cultures where difficult relationship issues such as loss or conflict make long-term decision making difficult.

Unique Mission Components

It is important in a family church to identify the unique ministries of that congregation. One transition strategy is for a transition consultant to meet with key members of the congregation and work through a process of naming all the key traditions in the church, prioritizing them, and documenting them in detail. The transition consultant would then meet with the former pastor and work through the same process. A comparison of the two would disclose which traditions are fully owned by the congregation and woven into the fabric of the congregation's life and which are more connected to the previous pastor and can be gently let go.

Asset Transfer

Asset transfer in a family culture can be handled in several ways, two of which are a bridging resource (such as an interim pastor or lay person with a checklist, like the one in Chapter Ten, who meets with the departing pastor and then briefs the arriving pastor at the end of the interim period) and a meeting between the departing pastor and the new pastor (moderated by an interim pastor, lay leader, or regional church official).

Advance Planning

Family cultures may be resistant to advance planning. This is especially true of a pastoral transition in a small congregation that is relationally based and has all the emotional qualities of a death. Just as we don't plan how and when a family member is going to die, it is emotionally impossible to plan far in advance a pastor's leaving. Here, the traditional wisdom holds. A pastor should let a congregation know that he or she is leaving shortly before the actual departure.

In larger family cultures, advance planning can be extremely helpful. These cultures can benefit from efforts to deepen the capability and maturity of the congregation (Chapter Eleven). Through a deliberate effort to increase the bench strength of the church's leadership, pastoral transition can be less traumatic and serve as an opportunity to broaden the church's understanding of ministry. Since it is extremely difficult for a large church in a family culture to adopt a new family leader effectively, a replication culture pastor with an understanding of family system dynamics may be a good successor to a family culture pastor.

Whatever the size of the church, *generic transition planning* for a family culture is possible. A generic transition plan outlines all the tasks required of the leadership in a transition, without specific reference to a timetable for the pastor's departure. Generally it contains many of the core elements of a "crisis transition plan" (Chapter Twelve) but without the traumatic and emergency dimensions. Church leaders should be clear about several points:

- The pastor's leaving can be expected to be sudden. Therefore, the leadership should be *ready* for the event when it comes.
- Both pastor and board generally agree that a long-term discussion of a pastoral departure is not appropriate in a family culture. A generic transition plan is the preferable approach.
- Transition consultants should be identified annually. This assistance may be compensated or it may be volunteered. Either way, it is critical that when the moment comes the leadership knows where to find the highest-qualified, most experienced assistance available. The consultants should be contacted in advance to check availability on a provisional basis. If they don't understand what you are doing in working on this in advance, they are not qualified to help you. Move on to the next person on the list.

If the pastor is functioning well, a pastoral retention plan should be in place. This plan should contain all seven elements found in the discussion of retention plans in Chapter Two. A good retention plan not only helps avoid unnecessary and costly leadership transitions but is a great selling point in recruiting a new pastor.

How It Could Be

The pastor had been at First Church about seven years when she began to reflect seriously on how to sustain the church across the pastoral transition once she moved on. She had no plans to make a move but felt the conviction of her responsibility to care for the church beyond her tenure as a matter of good stewardship. She had been faithful to First Church and endeared herself to the church family. It took her a number of years to be accepted, but after a flood hit the community and she had an opportunity to demonstrate her leadership and care for the people she was in like Flynn. She loved them, and they loved her.

Over her tenure to date, she was instrumental in developing new ministries, building the staff, reducing the debt on the property, and renovating fellowship hall. Worship attendance and membership were on the upswing. However, she had seen many churches like this one flourish under a pastor and then nearly founder under the burden of a surprise resignation. The big question in her mind was how to create a transition plan that would carry First Church through a pastoral transition without losing much of the momentum she had worked so hard to build.

She thought long and hard about how to introduce the topic of a pastoral transition plan to her leaders. She began by putting in their hands a videotape resource explaining how the former model for pastoral change was no longer effective. Then she explained (honestly) that she had no plans to leave the church, but that it only made sense for the church to have a generic plan that would describe step by step what should happen when a change took place. This could also serve as a crisis plan, she pointed out, because the unexpected was always a possibility. It would help her to feel better as a pastor, she told them, if she knew that they were taken care of if something were to happen to her.

The leadership appointed a transition planning committee, which took about three months to do its work. The plan included these elements:

- An interim pastor as a bridging resource who would take major responsibility for pastoral care and administration. A list of interims was obtained, and one was interviewed just to get a sense of what an interim does.
- A member of the congregation who was an outstanding speaker and respected by the congregation would preach twice a month. The church leaders put this in the plan because they knew that morale was related to preaching and their current pastor was an excellent preacher.
- An assessment of unique mission components. The leadership decided that there were three: (1) the after-school midweek

education program; (2) completion of the debt reduction campaign in three years; and (3) the youth music program, which went on the road for two weeks every spring.

• A definition of how the asset transfer would take place. The leadership would arrange a meeting between the departing pastor and the interim to have a pastor-to-pastor debrief. A checklist would be developed to facilitate this exchange of information. The same leader facilitating the meeting would then meet with the new pastor and the interim to make sure that the information was accurately transferred.

• Selection of their transition consultant. They went to their regional agency and asked for the best, most experienced person in that body to help them with their transition planning.

The generic pastoral transition plan was completed in about three months. It was reviewed annually and had no timelines. Both pastor and board decided that in their particular family culture dealing with a pastoral departure two years in advance was emotionally impossible. Besides, there are few secrets in a family. Two years later, the pastor announced that she had taken a call to Grace Church in another state. She would be leaving in eight weeks. Fortunately, a transition plan had been developed and was immediately brought on line.

The transition ideas put forth within it, along with the strength and commitment of the church leaders, are what sustained First Church during the transition. They called an interim pastor who could help the church experience its grief at the loss of the pastor, but also to look forward to who the next pastor would be. The pastoral transition planning committee became the transition team and worked closely with the interim pastor, the search committee, and the higher ups in accumulating and preparing the right data for the process to follow. They contacted the transition consultant they had identified two years before, who was skillful in helping them manage their transition. The interim served for about fourteen months while the search process was taking place. At last, a new pastor was on the way.

The transition team arranged for the interim pastor to remain for two months following the arrival of the new pastor. This gave enough time for the interim pastor to transfer the assets of knowledge to the new pastor, and to help him become acquainted with the family culture, as well as the community surrounding First Church. Unique mission components, so valued by the church, are being carried skillfully by the new pastor. After about four years, he is beginning to feel accepted.

What happened to the pastor at First Church ultimately happens to all pastors at some point in their careers. What happened with the actions of developing a pastoral transition plan almost never happens in a church. The model of the interim pastor is but one of many that can work during a time of transition. What is significant is that there was a plan that would bridge the gap of transition, and the leaders worked the plan and moved forward in a positive way.

Exhibit 5.1.

Transition at a Glance: Family Culture

Features

- Assumes configuration of family or tribe
- Provides continuity in local traditions and rituals
- Family systems usually smaller in scale but also include some larger multistaff churches
- May have strong boundaries that make it difficult for some people and pastors to get in

Language

- Reflects familial relationships: church as family, members are brothers or sisters
- Pastor is leader in family, as patriarch or matriarch, elder brother or elder sister

(Continued)

Exhibit 5.1. Continued.

Values

- Shared history, longevity, pedigree, respect, loyalty, local traditions, obedience, insiders, family unit, children, storytelling, practical service, sacrifice, duty, informality and being together.
- Penalizes or is passive toward an emphasis on effectiveness, strategic thinking, discontinuous change, methods, formal processes, experts, credentials, measuring, benchmarking, and outsiders

Transition Strategies

- Delayed arrival
    Interim pastor
    Lay professional
    Skilled volunteer
- Sequential timing
- Division of responsibility
- Unique mission components
- Asset transfer

Advance Planning

- Small family cultures and sudden departures
- Large family cultures and increasing congregational maturity and capability
- Generic transition planning

Chapter Six

Transition Strategies for Leaders in an Icon Culture

All the saints send you greetings, especially those
who belong to Caesar's household.
                    —*Philippians 4:22 (NIV)*

An *icon culture* is driven by the idea that a person can serve as a symbolic representation of the entire ministry of a church. The person becomes the public doorway through which people have access to the church and identify with the church's work. This is accomplished through a strong public presence, often amplified through the media—television, radio, CD, DVD, Internet. The person's face, voice, and name personalize a large organization and make it accessible to the community as a source of inspiration and grace.

Rather than shrinking from building a church around a personality, an icon culture fully capitalizes upon a leader's charismatic qualities as the primary means to advance the mission of the church. An icon culture knows that the public may not remember the name of a church, its denominational affiliation, or even its location; but they will remember the name and face of its leader. The leader's name is prominent in much of what the church does. It appears in newspapers and on television, buses, church signs, publications, advertisements, billboards, and bulletins. This emphasis on a personality means that pastoral transition involves a significant process of decoupling the ministry from the previous leader and recoupling it to a new one.

Other church cultures may look askance at placing this much emphasis on a single individual, but an icon culture realizes that the leader's personality is no more the center of the church's life than a door is equivalent to the building. Icons are merely doorways to a larger reality. No one mistakes a computer icon for the actual program. By the same token, an icon is the primary way the church's program is accessed and actualized.

On the surface, it may appear that icon cultures are superficial or shallow. A closer look may reveal a ministry of surprising depth. Behind the icon is often a church with a rich and extensive ministry that includes social services; religious schools and day care centers; after-school programs; fellowship structures; training seminars and clinics; high-quality educational programs; innovative children, youth, young adult, adult, and senior adult ministries; healing ministries; and support groups for people facing a range of traumas and illnesses. In addition to a host of local ministries, icon cultures may offer a range of international hands-on mission opportunities.

Since the burden of marketing, media, and production costs require economies of scale, icon cultures tend to be found in larger churches that the icon has been instrumental in building. Since they differ significantly from the religious environment in which most people grow up, icon cultures require a body of specialized, technical expertise that is not within the purview of many. This makes an icon church more dependent upon a specialized professional staff with a high degree of market savvy and sophistication. As a result, there is often a barrier between icon and other church cultures that makes it difficult to relate to the realm of celebrity and performance.

Icon cultures may also capitalize upon the celebrity status of their leader by connecting with other celebrities who have a spiritual story to tell. It is common for them to bring to their stage not just significant religious figures but also well-known political, entertainment, and sports personalities. Music in this culture is often concert-grade, as a worthy complement to the communication gifts of the leader.

Language in an icon culture tends to run on a double track. On one track is the language presented to the public, containing a vocabulary that is shaped around such personal spiritual categories as grace, love, sin, prayer, devotion, faith, forgiveness, purpose, abundance, joy, strength, eternal life, comfort, truth, insight, hope, and personal relationship with God. On the second track is the language required by the technical requirements of the culture. This includes a vocabulary that includes market, market share, market penetration, ratings, systems, structure, information technology, tracking, cost-effectiveness, return on investment, networking, make-up, lighting, staging, and so on. Missing from the public language of icon cultures are religious words of a more institutional nature, and references to issues affecting the local congregation or the denomination of which the church is a part. Sermons may also have a double track, with the section of the sermon that is televised geared toward a universal audience but with an untelevised segment for the "family."

An icon culture is a creative, entrepreneurial environment. It focuses on new and more effective ways of expressing the message. Pastors in icon cultures may be highly intuitive and can often anticipate and prepare for changes in society before they happen. This sometimes gives one the impression that they can tell the future—which places them on the cutting edge of a number of issues, particularly relating to communication. Because their followers come to trust this second sight, they can become highly dependent upon their leader. This means that transitional strategies have to work hard at finding a creative successor and at building trust between the new leader and the people.

The values of an icon culture tend to reward technical expertise, sophistication, attractiveness, dramatic experience, verbal expression, high-profile connections, stage presence, musical talent, artistic skill, graphic design, marketing, packaging, presentation, innovation, creativity, risk taking, gifts of preaching or teaching or healing, style, fashion, extraversion, wit, humor, spontaneity, and novelty. The values of an icon culture tend to penalize or are passive toward introversion, the mundane, mysticism, sacrament, abstract conceptual thinking, uncertainty, ambiguity, failure, struggle, plain looks, the outdated, and so on.

Leadership Transition Advantages

There are four leadership transition advantages of an icon culture:

1. The position is public and prestigious. It affords a single person an opportunity to influence thousands or even millions of lives.
2. Icon cultures generate significant revenue and expect to yield ample compensation for their leader.
3. Icon leaders wield significant power and are not hamstrung by intricate decision-making processes in the organization.
4. Icon leaders often stay in a particular church until they retire or initiate a new ministry elsewhere. This often brings some flexibility to their departure and opportunities to nurture and mentor a successor.

Risks in Choosing a Candidate

Probably no church has more at stake in a transition than one in an icon culture. An icon culture may have nearly as much organizational maturity in its ranks as a replication culture, but without that key public presence it cannot hold its audience while engaged in a prolonged search. It does not have the stability of an archival culture, which is built around history and liturgy rather than a personality. It does not have the relatively low-stakes (though painful) loss of a parental figure of the family church with an impact on a few dozen people, as opposed to thousands or millions.

Because icon cultures are relatively new on the historical scene, there are few resources available to assist them on their lonely road.

Denominational churches and structures are primarily concerned with small congregations, and their expertise tends to be focused on small-scale organizational structures. In addition, the public eye can be an extremely critical one. We do not tolerate well flaws in public figures or missteps in their decision making.

The selection risks borne by an icon culture are more similar to the risks run by a large corporation in selecting a chief executive officer than the risks incurred by most churches in selecting a new pastor. This is because the CEOs of many large corporations must have a strong public relations side to their work in addition to the significant internal leadership skills required by their position. These risks include:

- Lack of strategic thinking on the part of the church leadership that provides the criteria for a good selection process for a new CEO.
- A "find a star" mentality that overlooks the importance of a broad match of the leader to the organization's needs, rather than hiring a celebrity who was very successful in one context but might not be in another.
- A pastor who undermines or controls the search process for a successor.
- Candidates who are so enamored of the prestige of the job that they do not soberly evaluate the fit of their person to the whole of the position.
- Failure of key leaders to invest adequately in the difficult work of finding a successor to an unusually gifted individual—in a word, laziness.
- Failure of search consultants to do a thorough job in helping the church set specifications, screen applicants, and assist with the transition process.
- Inexperience on the part of those involved in the transition and search process. Generally, the key leadership has never served in another church (especially not in an icon culture) or been involved in a leadership transition of this magnitude. At the

very moment that expert leadership is needed, leaders are at the bottom of a steep learning curve.

All of these risks can be managed, but doing so requires a skilled and dedicated transition team vested with adequate authority to do the job, coupled with adequate external resources.

Critical Transition Tasks

There are a number of critical transition tasks, most of which are articulated in Chapter Three. But several need to be emphasized.

First, as a church enters into a transition process, it is important for the leadership to enter into a time of study and prayer. Though much of this book focuses on transition strategies, it is important to keep clearly in mind that the church is God's church, and He is to take the lead through the transition process. As the leadership of the church looks to God for direction, all of the strategizing, planning, networking, and the like will connect wonderfully. Without entrusting the process to Him and leaning on Him for direction, all of the best laid plans of men and women may not bear the desired fruit in the end.

Second, a pastoral transition in an icon culture requires the resources of a professional search consultant who is external to the church itself. It is likely that there are powerful personalities with strong opinions in the church involved in the transition. This requires that the search consultant be skilled, experienced, and well-grounded. Finding the right consultant can be a challenge in itself, since there are few. However, it would be wise to look for someone who understands the Christian faith *and* who clearly understands the personality of the local church, its style of ministry (conservative, liberal, evangelical, fundamentalist, charismatic), and its ministries and vision. Having that knowledge, the consultant can narrow the field of search. This is where the ability to network can reduce the length of time for a search.

Third, the public nature of the icon culture may require the services of a qualified public relations firm. This depends largely on the scope and breadth of the ministry that is beyond the local church. If the pastor's ministry has spread nationally or internationally via television, writing, speaking, and so on, then a public relations specialist should be involved in preparing proper and adequate communication to the public regarding the departure of the pastor and transition to a new one.

Fourth, a transition team fully empowered by the board should be put in place to manage the transition. There should be a clear delineation of responsibilities assigned to the board, the transition team, the consultants, and the departing pastor. This transition team might consist of eight to ten leaders who are mature in their faith, understand the full ministry of the church, are trustworthy and dependable, and are willing to commit whatever amount of time it takes to complete the task. Selecting this team requires thought and diligent prayer.

Fifth, the public and private passing of the baton is critical and should be carefully managed. Anyone who has watched a relay race knows that the race is often won or lost by how well the baton is passed. This is especially true in an icon culture. All of the planning that goes into transition must be sustained through the hand-off of the baton and into the early stages of the new pastor's term. This must include the graceful exit of the departing pastor and the welcome of the new pastor, and all of what goes with those steps behind the scenes.

Any ongoing role of the departing pastor should be carefully defined and bounded. Many new pastors are anxious about a resident predecessor not staying within appropriate boundaries and that the board will not hold the departing pastor accountable for those violations. One impetus for compliance would be a clause in the new pastor's contract awarding a financial sum to the pastor in the event that the departing pastor does not comply with specified boundaries. Although rarely enforced (hopefully), the clause sends a clear message to all parties that these boundaries are taken seriously.

Threats to the Success of the New Pastor

Like the family culture, the primary transition threat in an icon culture is loyalty conflict. Because an icon culture constructs the church's identity around a personality, the transfer of loyalty to a new leader is difficult. In contrast to a family culture, the loyalty is not to an actual person, but to the icon. Externally, the discussion points for the loyalty transfer involve stage presence, communication skills, authenticity, physical attractiveness, and spiritual clarity. Internally, the discussion points for the loyalty transfer are on vision, leadership, and staff development.

The shadow transitional threat in an icon culture is a demand for relationship. This is because icon cultures tend to value the media image of a leader and the need to market that image. It may be difficult for them to admit that they need something more grounded in reality and more attuned to grace in the ordinary. Denying this need threatens to become a shadow within the organization that members want to avoid or deny. An icon culture may desperately need more ordinary grace but may not honor it in a successor.

Transition Strategies

The transition strategy that works best in a family culture, delayed arrival, is a disaster in an icon culture. This is because the public nature of the culture demands a new icon as the doorway to the church in order to stay engaged. Icon cultures cannot endure several months of substandard worship leadership while the church looks for a successor. Therefore it is important to plan for an overlap between the departing pastor and his or her successor. This is an opportunity for the departing pastor to pass the mantle to the successor. There are several overlap options that should be considered:

• *Promotion of an internal candidate.* Since icon cultures are relatively rare, a gifted internal staff member could be a good candidate to be promoted to pastor. This approach has the advantage of affording a candidate significant in-house experience in the culture and exposure to the staff, and perhaps the public. A candidate with a good track record in the internal arena, with appropriate gifts to serve in the public arena, can build confidence in his or her ability to be effective. The downside of this approach is that serving in any other level of the organization is not the same as being the leader. The only way to learn how to be an executive leader is to be mentored and serve as an executive leader. If the opportunity has not been provided, the leader has not yet been truly tested.

- *Off-stage mentor.* In this approach, the former pastor serves as an offstage mentor to an externally recruited candidate. This approach has the advantage that the candidate can have gained some executive leader experience in a previous assignment. It creates an opportunity for the candidate to be mentored by the previous pastor without confusing the public about who is really in charge.

- *Co-pastor.* In the co-pastor approach, an external candidate is called to share in the pastor duties with the departing pastor. The responsibilities are split as evenly as possible, with equal compensation and title. Gradually over a period of several months, the departing pastor is phased out through a "practiced absence." This approach has the advantage of calling a candidate with executive leadership experience.

- *Family member.* The icon can designate a son or daughter as successor. This can be criticized as capitulation to privilege, but a case could be made for the legitimacy of the option. The evidence is now strong that about 50 percent of our personality traits can be attributed to genetics. Since the effectiveness of an icon culture is so dependent on the personality of the icon, it follows that a logical choice might be a son or daughter of the icon. Care must be exercised to ensure that the person has the gifts and training necessary for the task and is not automatically considered to be heir to the throne.

There are other aspects of the transition to consider:

- *Training.* It is critical for the new pastor to understand the dynamics of an icon culture. This may require mentoring from the departing pastor, coaching from a transition team, or more formal training in the fields of marketing and communication.
- *Public relations.* As has been mentioned, it is also important that the public passing of the baton be handled well. The choice of a firm that understands the religious community is important and should be made well in advance.
- *Staff management.* Since the staff in an icon culture often possesses an unusual set of skills, it is important to implement a program of staff retention in the transition process. The board must work proactively to staunch any talent drain that may be threatened during the transition.

Advance Planning

Advance planning is critical for a successful pastoral transition in an icon culture. When establishing a time line, the governing board in an icon culture should consider the multiple components and complexity of the transition, the challenge involved in finding a viable successor, and the need to manage both the public dimension of the transition and the congregational dimension of the transition. All of these considerations point to the need to begin incorporating transition planning with strategic planning at least three to five years in advance of the pastor's anticipated departure. If time is short in a situation, it is never too late to begin to plan along the lines discussed here.

How It Could Be

Lakeview Church ran a good race from the start. The pastor had built a strong and diverse ministry over a long period of time. Not only did the church double in size many times over, it became well-known around the country. The visionary pastor never ran out of new ideas, new ministries, or new concepts for spreading the Word. Lakeview's television ministry triggered the pastor to write books and develop a ministry completely beyond Lakeview Church. In time, Lakeview's pastor was considered a major religious spokesperson in the country. The pastor developed into an icon.

As with everything in life, there is a season. The season for transition came to Lakeview. About three or so years prior to the pastor's departure, he began to discuss his exit plans with the personnel committee. After a lengthy period of time seeking the Lord's guidance, talking with a consultant, exploring all possible options, and processing all the information with the church board, it was decided that the leadership of the church would seek a co-pastor to share the ministry for several months. On the departure of the pastor, the co-pastor would continue as the senior pastor of the church.

With that decision made, the appointed transition team went to work designing and executing a health-based plan for transition. As they began the process, they quickly realized how little they knew about transition and a search process. Though the church board and many church members were executives in the corporate world, none had any experience in pastoral transition of any kind. In fact, most of them had been members of Lakeview for more than ten years, so they were limited in their church history and experience.

They were quick to realize the uniqueness of Lakeview Church, in that it was a megachurch with megaministries, megastaff, a budget equal to a mid-sized business, a school, an expansive facility, property development concerns, television ministry, and more. They knew that managing these unique mission components during a time of transition would be critical. A transition team of nine people who were well acquainted with Lakeview and respected by the congregation was carefully and prayerfully constructed.

In the months that followed, this little "company of the committed" studied and prayed together, seeking God's will in all of their work, and as He led, they moved. They used all five key players (departing pastor, church board, personnel committee, arriving pastor, and transition consultant) at the appropriate times. They found a transition consultant who also functioned as a search consultant to be a wise investment, and the end result was that the new co-pastor arrived within thirty days of what was planned. The departing pastor slipped into the role of a paraclete, coming alongside the new pastor and sharing valuable information as the transfer of assets was completed.

At the end of about four months, a celebration was held, good-byes were said, and the pastor departed. The transition team continued to work with the new pastor for several months, until it was clear that its members were no longer needed. As they ended their time, there was a quiet celebration among the team as well as a time of rejoicing and thanking God for leading the process and guiding them safely across the transition. To this day, the members of the team continue to pray for the pastor. The baton was smoothly passed.

Exhibit 6.1.

Transition at a Glance: Icon Culture

Features

- A person symbolizes an entire ministry with prominence of name, face, voice
- Capitalizes on charismatic qualities of the leader
- Often has significant behind-the-scene ministries to people in need
- Tends to be large to capture economies of scale
- Networks to other celebrities and uses their stories to advance the mission

Language

- Tends to run on a double track
- On one track: personal spiritual categories such as grace, love, sin, prayer, devotion, faith, forgiveness, purpose, abundance, joy, strength, eternal life, comfort, truth, insight, hope, and personal relationship with God

- On second track: technical requirements such as market, market share, market penetration, ratings, systems, structure, information technology, tracking, cost-effectiveness, return on investment, networking, make-up, lighting, staging, and so on

Values

- The values of an icon culture tend to reward technical expertise, sophistication, attractiveness, dramatic experience, verbal expression, high profile, connections, stage presence, musical talent, artistic skill, graphic design, marketing, packaging, presentation, innovation, creativity, risk taking, gifts of preaching or teaching or healing, style, fashion, extraversion, wit, humor, spontaneity, and novelty.
- The values of an icon culture tend to penalize or are passive toward introversion, the mundane, mysticism, sacrament, abstract conceptual thinking, uncertainty, ambiguity, failure, struggle, plain looks, and the outdated.

Transition Advantages

- Resources and prestige of position make it attractive
- Opportunity to influence large numbers of people a significant recruitment factor

Transition Strategies

- Family member: the icon can designate a son or daughter as successor.
- Promotion of an internal candidate: since icon cultures are relatively rare, a gifted internal staff member could be a good candidate to be promoted to pastor.
- Off-stage mentor: in the co-pastor approach an external candidate is called to share in the pastoral duties with the departing pastor.

Other Aspects

- Training
- Public relations
- Staff management

Advance Planning

- Minimum three to five years' advance preparation prior to pastoral transition

Chapter Seven

Transition Strategies for Leaders in an Archival Culture

So then, brothers, stand firm and hold to the
teachings we passed on to you, whether by word
of mouth or by letter.

—*II Thessalonians 2:15 (NIV)*

An archival culture is driven by the idea that the church is the repository of wisdom that has accumulated over the ages. The seminal ideas are ancient and may constitute a drama that is reenacted as a means of participation and revitalization. The reenactment takes the form of a liturgy that is highly stylized. The Passover epitomizes this culture, with its liturgical reenactment of an historical event and broad, multigenerational participation. Leaders in this culture may not be defined principally in terms of programs, relationships, or preaching skill but rather in their role as sustainer of a core of traditions and a central, defining drama. This core of traditions stands in front of the leader. As a result, a leadership transition tends to be a secondary impact compared to a change in the theology or practice of the liturgy that would be primary and redefining.

An archival culture is driven by the knowledge of the tradition that sustains the culture. This knowledge comprises a large and significant compendium of information, including core beliefs and affirmations, central liturgical texts and formats, construction and furnishing of worship space, choreography of the worship experience, roles and relationships of leaders at various levels within the hierarchy, seasonal celebrations and variations, and the historical precedents that are the foundation of church praxis. The assimilation of this substantial informational content requires a long, standardized education process that tends to regularize leaders at the point of initiation.

What the replication culture seeks to accomplish at the level of the laity (standardized training with core beliefs, values, skills, and commitments among a growing body of leaders) the archival culture achieves at the level of the ordained professional. Leaders may diverge in their views with the passage of time, but this standardization of content tends to make a leadership transition less disruptive.

A second idea that drives the archival culture is the universality of the experience. This includes continuity not just across time (as has already been noted) but also across space. Vigorous compliance with the web of church thinking and doing produces a synchronicity that transcends local, regional, and national identities. Members of an archival culture are strengthened by knowing that their experience of the church in any other part of the world will share in the same rhythms, values, expressions, and reenactments that they experience in their local community. This continuity across time and space brings a deep sense of being at home in the universe. As a result, members of an archival culture may be ready to accept a less localized and customized religious experience in order to appreciate a broader sense of belonging. As the drive for localization and customization recedes, the magnitude of the transition from leader to leader decreases as well.

A third idea that drives the archival culture is the need for a strong, centralized, and hierarchical government that holds enough power to ensure that the universal nature of its life and mission are not sacrificed to the vagaries of the local community. Therefore, in contrast to many Protestant traditions, substantial power does not rest in the local congregation itself but rather in the governing system above the local congregation and those acting on behalf of that governing system. Since the power to select, train, and place leaders is critical for compliance with the tradition in all its various expressions, members of local congregations in archival cultures accept the fact that their leaders are chosen *for* them and not *by* them. This is not to say that some members of archival cultures may not desire more say in these transitions. But generally they find that the strength of the culture prevails over these sentiments. This means that the transitional strategies that are most effective are those that acknowledge these cultural realities and work consonantly across the grid of values that drive these systems.

The language of an archival culture often reflects the orientation of the culture to its history. Sometimes this takes the form of a liturgy that is intentionally and completely nonvernacular (such as the Latin mass). Sometimes the liturgy retains the language of an immigrant population even after the assimilation of that population into a regional culture complete with another language. Even short of these more extreme cases, archival cultures tend to borrow heavily from antecedent cultures and languages for the nomenclature of their liturgical components.

Language in an archival culture creates a significant boundary for the community, which enables it to retain a sense of identity amid a chaotic or challenging world. Even renewal movements within archival communities tend to develop their own vocabulary according to the historical context in which the movements began. As an example, the Cursillo movement in the Roman Catholic Church makes extensive use of a Spanish vocabulary since the movement originated in that historical context.

The emphasis on a religious language that is essentially a second language to the vernacular is an additional informational requirement placed upon a leader. (It may actually be a fourth language when consideration is given to the requirement to know the Hebrew and Greek of original sacred texts as well.) When we say that an archival culture is knowledge-driven, the knowledge of languages beyond the vernacular is a significant informational requirement. Again, this is a force in the direction of standardized leadership, which lessens the impact of a leadership transition.

Archival culture churches tend to vary in size, from small parishes in isolated regions to urban and suburban parishes with hundreds of families. Unlike replication cultures, where size requires a different training strategy, or family cultures, where size can be a threat to intimacy, archival cultures are much more adaptive to changes of scale. Parishes can grow or shrink by simply adding or removing a liturgy that is nearly a clone of the first. This makes scale changes more easily traversed in an archival culture and less difficult for leaders moving from one scale to the next.

An archival culture tends to be maintenance-focused. Leaders in this culture have a greater tendency to be introverted than in the other church cultures, which means they draw energy from their inner world of thoughts and ideas. They also tend to be focused on details and concrete operations. In standard personality testing, three times as many Roman Catholic priests are introverted sensors as pastors from other cultures. This means they base their ideas on a deep, solid accumulation of stored impressions, which gives them some pretty unshakable ideas. No type is more thorough, painstaking, systematic, hardworking, or patient with detail or routine. Pastoral transition in an archival culture needs to honor this need for dependability by providing the information necessary for a new pastor to be successful in maintaining the order of things.

The values of an archival culture tend to reward historical precedent, initiation, longevity, pedigree, respect, loyalty, global continuity, order, obedience, ritual, continuity, structure, universality, sacrifice, duty, sharp role definition, formality, and credential. The values of an archival culture tend to penalize (or treat passively) an emphasis on effectiveness, uniqueness, autonomy, change, measurement, benchmarking, spontaneity, adaptation, and porous boundaries to outsiders. In other church cultures, it may be much more difficult to enter the church as a leader (with hours of document preparation, interviews, sermon taping, site visits, multiple votes by different governing bodies, and so on) than to enter the church as a new member (which may take place at the end of a worship service). In an archival culture, by contrast, it is often more difficult to enter the culture as a new member (with months of classes) than to enter it as a leader (a relatively simple appointment process). Archival cultures may emphasize the need for entire families to enter the culture rather than individuals, and they may refuse applicants certain experiences or status depending upon the disposition of other family members. With these significant boundaries in place, archival cultures tend to have less operational diversity than other cultures; this tends to homogenize expectations and make leadership transition less traumatic.

Leadership Transition Advantages

Of all cultures, the archival are the most resilient in the face of a pastoral transition. As one Roman Catholic lay leader said in his interview, "The pastoral transition is one of the healthiest things we do." There are four leadership transition advantages of an archival culture:

1. The central experience of the culture, the liturgy, is shaped by history, not by the innovation of the pastor. In a real sense, the culture has an unchangeable liturgy with an interchangeable pastor (whereas other cultures tend to have interchangeable liturgies with unchangeable pastors).

2. The universality of the religious experience tends to discourage "church shopping" in the face of a pastoral change. In the ideal archival culture, the worship experience at Parish A is nearly identical to that at Parish B regardless of the pastoral leadership. Some people may move to another parish because of a programmatic emphasis beyond the liturgy, but it is the liturgy that serves as the defining experience for the majority of persons.

3. Because an archival culture tends to have an appointed system that places leaders rather than calling them, the transition

period can be short or nonexistent. This reduces the chaos and uncertainty found in the long transition of a family culture.

4. The seasonal programmatic rhythms of an archival culture tend to be prescribed (from within the hierarchy), including special offerings, mission emphasis, and the timing of certain sacraments. This gives a more universal, nonlocal ambiance to the church that is less dependent on a local pastor.

This is not to deny that significant power is given to local leaders in an archival community. Pastors may have significant impact in developing new administrative structures such as committees or task forces. They may institute new mission emphases locally or internationally. However, pastors tend not to be entrepreneurial in reaching people in their community. If an archival parish is growing, this is generally because the community around it is growing with people who are historically archival in background.

For these reasons, archival communities are not only more immune to the upheavals experienced by other church cultures in transition; they are less troubled by the boundary issues between previous and present leaders that often arise in the other cultures. It is not unusual for an archival culture to move a pastor to a new assignment only a few miles away. In other church cultures, this would generate significant anxiety about members of the flock moving from one parish to another in order to stay with their pastor. Because the focus of an archival culture is on the common liturgical experience that is grounded in history rather than shaped around the leader, this threat is greatly reduced. It is also not unusual for past leaders in archival cultures to return to lead worship, conduct weddings and funerals, or even serve in an assistant role in the case of retirement. In nonarchival cultures this would be extremely threatening to the current pastor, where even simple social contact may be forbidden between members and former leaders.

Although members of archival cultures may read these advantages as overstating the case in light of their own experience, it is important to realize that we tend to assess our experience relative to our own cultural context. Exceptions can be found in which local factors have made for a particularly traumatic transition in an archival culture. We would argue that, on the whole, leadership transitions in these cultures tend to be less disruptive to the system as well as to the emotional and spiritual fabric of the community.

Risks in the Appointment Process

Since the pastor in an archival culture is typically appointed to a local parish, there is no opportunity for the parish to make a faulty decision regarding the next pastor. The risks for the archival church move up the line to the larger system that recruits, trains, and places pastoral leadership. A system that is maintenance-focused may be attractive to a smaller population of personality types. To use the Myers-Briggs Type Indicator, we would say leaders in archival systems tend to be more introverted and fact-based than in other religious cultures, where leaders tend to be more extraverted and vision-based. Other strictures that serve the needs of the institution, such as celibacy (single pastors have more time to devote to the needs of the church and require smaller compensation) further reduce the population of possible candidates. In addition, those who do respond may not find avenues for expression of the creative, entrepreneurial, or generative side of their personality, with a resultant sapping of vital energy.

A major transition risk in an archival system is a restricted pool of candidates leading to a poor match between parish and pastor. Archival cultures can lower their expectations of pastoral leadership, which then become normative within the culture. What the archival system gains at the local level in minimizing disruption during transition, it may lose at higher levels in the vocational transition from lay person to pastor, where too few candidates are available to serve the church and creative individuals are discouraged from service.

Although these critical issues in the archival culture are beyond the scope of this book, the scarcity of leadership in the broader culture is an issue for all churches and all church cultures. It is well documented in the secular literature that leadership is at a premium today. This scarcity is a partial explanation for the high salaries commanded by CEOs of large corporations. Management expert Peter Drucker argues that leading a large church today is one of the three toughest jobs in the United States (along with university president and hospital executive). Laypeople often underestimate the complexity of pastoral leadership. The low pay and spiritual dimensions of the work lull them into a false belief that what is primarily required is good intention and hard work. There is a significant skill set required for church leadership, a skill set that takes years to develop.

If there are an inadequate number of candidates in the leadership pool, all churches are forced to make leadership choices that are less than optimal. What appears on the surface to be a transition problem may in fact be a leadership development problem in the Kingdom as a whole. Every church culture needs to be about the long-term business of stewarding leadership. This stewardship has several key components:

- A clear vision for the role of the church in the world that is vital and compelling.

- A vision for leadership that provides avenues for expression of the whole self and the range of gifts that people bring to the world.

- A systematic approach to leadership development that is built on the large body of leadership research currently available and recognizes the various kinds of leadership needed at different organizational levels.

- A means of retaining gifted leaders through re-recruitment and support.

Archival systems must manage significant placement risks. For many, the ideal archival culture might minimize localization and customization at the congregational level and make pastoral leaders largely interchangeable. In reality, local distinctions do exist among archival congregations, and they make some pastoral matches better than others. If those who are responsible for the appointive process do not have a systematic way to assess a congregation in terms of its spiritual, strategic, and operational needs, a suboptimal pastoral match will occur.

Critical Transition Tasks

The two critical transition tasks in an archival church are role definition and tradition continuity. Functionally, there is some latitude in how pastors choose to define their role, the degree to which they are willing to delegate to others, and the extent of their adherence to standard procedures. It is helpful if new leaders in archival systems are clear about their role with their new congregation and its leaders so that expectations can be set at an appropriate level and people are helped to be successful from the outset.

As in the family culture, tradition continuity promotes consistency in the rituals and traditions that are the key to the archival culture's well-being. Here there is a double tradition. There is the historic tradition that is universal and accepted, but there are local traditions as well that must be supported and sustained. It is helpful if the new leader takes the initiative to become familiar with these local traditions so that he or she can support them appropriately.

Threats to Success

The primary transition threat in an archival culture is not leadership. The greater threat is a liturgical, theological, and ethical transition. Any perceived discontinuity between the church's practice and its historic stance constitutes a major disruption in the life of the culture. The issue of using Latin in the mass continues to be controversial in certain quarters of the church long after a change in official church policy. Because an archival culture requires that people be loyal to a set of ideas, members feel conflicted if a new set of ideas suddenly emerges on the scene to which they now must give assent and adapt. Change in an archival culture tends to occur at a much slower pace than in other church cultures.

The shadow transitional threat in an archival culture is a hunger for vitality. This is because the culture tends to value conformity and maintenance functions and devalue innovation, spontaneity, and entrepreneurial initiative. However, there is a degree of creativity, spontaneity, and conflict that is necessary for vitality and growth. Denying this need threatens to become a shadow within the organization that members want to avoid or deny. If this need is not surfaced and honored, the vitality of the parish may suffer.

A second shadow transitional threat in an archival culture is the need for relationship. The abrupt movement of leaders in and out of a congregation emphasizes the durability of the church's traditions and the universal quality of its core values. However, the bond between leader and people is relational in nature, not merely strategic or operational. Some leadership transitions can be painful for congregations, and all are experienced as a loss. If processes are not put in place to allow people to surface and process their grief, emotional and spiritual wounds may sabotage a transitional program that is otherwise functionally exquisite.

Transition Strategies

• Develop an annual process for assessing the state of the church, the state of the local community, and current pastoral and programmatic needs. This information can not only guide the local body in its planning but also be submitted to regional authorities. This initiative, taken by the local church, can bring guidance to the appointment process.

- In every pastoral transition, have the local congregational leaders identify unique mission components to be shared with the arriving pastor (Chapter Ten).
- Conduct a pastor-to-pastor debrief after new appointments have been made (checklist in Chapter Ten).
- Build on the strengths of the archival system to manage the transition. Have the departing pastor and new pastor lead a transitional worship service together that emphasizes the universal qualities of the church's life and acknowledges loss, pain, and new possibilities at the same time.
- Develop a set of rituals, devotional materials, and transitional activities, based on the best research available, that can tend to the needs of people relating to loss, grief, and closure.
- Define any ongoing role of the departing pastor in the parish and the protocols for involvement.

At the level of regional bodies within archival systems:

- Develop a systematic means of assessing the vitality and distinct qualities of local congregations to guide the appointment process.
- Develop a consultant service with quality resources within the regional agency to guide local congregations in their transition planning and implementation.

Advance Planning

Archival systems are experiencing a renewal of vitality and numbers. In the Roman Catholic tradition, the growth in the number of congregants combined with a shortage of priests is placing stress on personnel and facilities. For these reasons, it is important for parish leaders to be strategic in their thinking about the future. A strategic plan for the local congregation, prepared in consultation with the regional authorities and under the guidance of the local leader, could be important in guiding both lay and clergy. Such a plan, updated annually, could set goals that unify the church around key activities.

Even though archival cultures are often appointed systems, they may have some limited degree of input regarding future transitions. In some archival cultures, appointments are made for a given term (six years, for example) with possible renewal for an additional term. In years of probable transition, the church can be proactive in communicating information to the appointing authority regarding the state of the church and its needs.

How It Could Be

St. Mary's Catholic Church is located in an older suburb of a medium-sized city. The community is essentially landlocked, and no appreciable increase in population has taken place there for more than twenty years.

The parish council takes an active role in the oversight of the parish, encouraged to do so by a priest who believes in collaborative decision making. Each year, the council engages in an annual assessment of the parish, and every three years it uses a standardized church survey to evaluate the health of the congregation. In the previous winter, it conducted the latest round of survey work and reviewed the results at the January meeting. The results indicated that the church was strong on indices relating to morale, faith centrality, and participatory decision making. It was somewhat weaker on openness to change and financial giving. The parish council has carefully reviewed the survey results and decided to set goals related to increased stewardship and special offerings for mission. The council sets goals such as these annually and sends them to the bishop as a way of keeping him abreast of what is happening at St. Mary's.

Father Vincent has been in the parish for twelve years; the policy of the diocese is to reassign after two six-year terms. Aware of this, the council has decided to give consideration to the kind of successor who would be helpful to the parish. They generated this list of attributes:

- A clear theology of giving and a means of increasing the giving of the parish

- Experience with mission, both local and international, that can serve as a resource to help St. Mary's move forward in that area

- The ability to manage change for this older parish where change is somewhat difficult

This list of attributes was submitted to the bishop for consideration as part of his discernment process in appointing the successor to Father Vincent.

In anticipation of Father Vincent's leaving, the parish council took a number of steps. The council members planned a series of events for the parish to say goodbye, including a photo scrapbook and dinner; they took up a collection to enable Father Vincent to take a trip to New Hampshire in the fall for a weeklong retreat; and they identified the five most important ministries of the parish that they considered unique and effective.

The new appointment to the parish was Monsignor McNeil. The parish worked with both pastors so that they could celebrate mass together on the last weekend of Father Vincent's ministry at St. Mary's. Father Vincent had learned enough about Monsignor McNeil that he could introduce him to the parish in some detail and with sincere affirmation.

In the week before the transition, both pastors met for a full day of pastor-to-pastor debrief. They covered a list of topics generated by Father Vincent. He spent a significant amount of time on the five most important ministries of the parish that the council had identified. He scheduled a lunch with the entire parish staff so that everyone would have an opportunity to meet with Monsignor McNeil in a relaxed atmosphere.

Since Father Vincent was being appointed to a parish less than three miles away, they agreed that he would be welcome to assist with funerals and weddings over the next year upon the invitation of Monsignor McNeil. They also agreed to jointly celebrate mass at the parish's one-hundredth anniversary the next spring.

Three years later, the annual church survey showed that giving had increased by about 20 percent under Monsignor's McNeil's leadership. The emphasis on mission was also fruitful, though the openness-to-change scores still indicate an older congregation that values its traditions and is slow to change. The parish council reported this information to the bishop in its annual report and continues to function constructively in an advisory role to all those in the church called to discern God's future.

Exhibit 7.1.

Transition at a Glance: Archival Culture

Features

- Church as repository of ancient wisdom reenacted in liturgy
- Universality of experience across time and space
- Strong, centralized hierarchical government to ensure universality

Language

- Reflects orientation to historical roots
- Multiple vocabularies

Values

- Rewards historical precedent, initiation, longevity, respect, loyalty, obedience, ritual, universality, sacrifice, duty, sharp role definition, formality, credentials
- Punishes or is passive toward emphasis on effectiveness, uniqueness, autonomy, measurement, benchmarking, spontaneity, adaptation, local control

Transition Advantages

- Unchangeable liturgy with interchangeable pastor
- Discourages "church shopping"
- Short transition periods
- Reduction of emphasis on single individual
- Less troubled by boundary issues between parishes

Transition Strategies

- Develop an annual process for assessing the state of the church, the state of the local community, and current pastoral and programmatic needs. This information can not only guide the local body in its planning but also be submitted to regional authorities. This initiative, taken by the local church, can bring guidance to the appointment process.
- In every pastoral transition, local congregational leaders identify unique mission components to be shared with the arriving pastor (Chapter Ten).
- Conduct a pastor-to-pastor debrief after new appointments have been made (Chapter Ten).
- Build on the strengths of the archival system to manage the transition. Have the departing pastor and new pastor lead a transitional worship service together that emphasizes the universal qualities of the church's life and acknowledges loss, pain, and new possibilities at the same time.
- Develop a set of rituals, devotional materials, and transitional activities based on the best research available that can tend to the needs of the people relating to grief and closure.
- Define any ongoing role of the departing pastor in the parish and the protocols for involvement.
- At the level of regional bodies within archival systems, develop a systematic means of assessing the vitality and distinct qualities of local congregations to guide the appointment process; and develop a consultant service with quality resources within the regional agency to guide local congregations in their transition planning and implementation.

Advance Planning

- Strategic issues related to growth in number of congregants and decrease in number of pastors.
- Cycle of pastoral appointments creates opportunity for communication with the appointing authority.

Chapter Eight

Transition Strategies for Leaders in a Replication Culture

> Whatever you have learned or received or heard
> from me, or seen in me—put it into practice.
> —*Philippians 4:9 (NIV)*

Two ideas drive an effective replication culture. The first is that leadership traits can be developed rather than simply inherited. Although truly great leaders have native gifts that bestow particular leadership capacities, many people can be developed as leaders given the right training approach and commitment. Research on leadership development indicates the validity of this concept particularly as it incorporates adult-learning principles (for example, participation of the adult learner in his or her own learning process, respect for the current knowledge base of the learner, opportunities for immediate application of learning, and connections among fields of knowledge). The implication of this idea for pastoral transitions is that a sophisticated, long-term adult training program must be developed years in advance of an anticipated pastoral transition.

The second idea of the replication culture is that effective leadership relies on a body of knowledge that can be transferred from one leader to another. Here we are using *knowledge* broadly so that it encompasses not only information but also skill development and attitude formation. This transfer places a particular burden on leaders in that they have the dual responsibility of leading as well as teaching, training, mentoring, and coaching. These all require distinct skill sets, and the number of people willing and able to do both well is not large. However, given visionary leadership from the top and sufficient commitment to this idea, combined with a large enough pool of members to create a critical mass, nearly any ministry can be replicated. This means that discerning the right people for the various levels of leadership within the organization is a critical task, especially if the next pastor will be recruited internally.

The vocabulary of a replication culture has a number of local variants, but it may focus on equipping, mentoring, coaching, reproducible, discipling, raising up, bench strength, leadership DNA, best practices, training, skill development, benchmarking, "teaching a person to fish" and teaching "as you walk on the way" (and "I do, you watch; we do, you do; I watch, you do"), capacity building, core competencies, and organizational maturity. The language tends to be shaped around the processes through which replication takes place.

The replication culture tends to be a thinking culture. Leaders are likely to make decisions on the basis of an objective set of principles, thoroughly and fairly applied. They can be avid readers of literature, secular and religious, which is their attempt to better understand how people and systems work. They may explore how their system of thinking applies to complex ethical and moral issues of the day. This makes the replication culture more likely to be successful in an educational environment than any other culture. Selecting and preparing successors must honor this thinking dimension of the personality and organization.

The values of a replication culture tend to reward standardized content and instructional methods, being teachable and trainable, levels of mastery, having followers, depth and bench strength, clarity, and internal recruitment. The values of a replication culture tend to penalize or are passive toward a "star mentality," person-centered leadership, dependency and paternalism, external recruitment of leadership, ambiguity (difficulty in communication and replication), and tradition.

Leadership Transition Advantages

A replication culture has a number of important advantages relating to pastoral transitions:

- They have significant experience with leadership transitions at lower levels of the organization. Since leadership in these churches tends to be upwardly mobile, members are familiar with the dynamics of these transitions and can extrapolate their experience to the senior pastor or leader.

- Replication cultures tend to have a solid leadership pool. These leaders can help carry the church during major leadership changes at the top of the organization.

- Replication cultures tend to promote from within so that the new leader is someone who is already known and who knows the people in the church. This eliminates many of the errors that occur as an incoming leader is trying to learn how to navigate in a new corporate culture.

- Replication cultures tend to focus more on leader effectiveness than on personality. Even though it is difficult to draw a sharp line between effectiveness and personality, emphasizing the effectiveness of the leader rather than the relationship with the leader tends to attenuate the interpersonal dimensions of grief that can paralyze other church cultures for years.

Leadership Transition Risks

Replication cultures have several risks relative to leadership transition that may result in selecting a less-qualified candidate:

- Lack of senior pastor experience. The leadership skills required by the senior leader are distinct from those at any other level of the organization. It is a mistake to think that one can learn these skills by functioning well at another level or by merely observing the senior pastor at work.

- The distortion created by internal competition. When a person in the church knows that he or she is being considered to be the senior leader, the pressure can cause disruption in relationships or other behavior that would not be typical in another setting. "Anger is cruel and fury overwhelming, but who can stand before jealousy?" (Proverbs 27:4 NIV).

- Replication churches run the risk of becoming ingrown. Because leadership is groomed internally, the organization may lack the cross-pollination of fresh ideas and perspectives that come from leaders of other churches.

These risks can be tempered by specific mentoring of the candidate by the departing pastor, spiritual and emotional support to internal candidates, external benchmarking, and seeking best practices.

Critical Transition Tasks

The critical transition task in a replication church is knowledge transfer. As has been mentioned, knowledge is understood in the broad sense of the word and includes information, or course, but also skill development and attitudinal formation. This knowledge transfer can include formal education, workshops, mentoring, briefings, and spiritual direction. The formidable task of training a pastor or leader can take five to twenty years depending on the maturity and capability of the candidate when he or she entered the church.

Some replication cultures are part of a polity structure that does not permit internal recruitment for the senior leader. If this is the case, an external candidate will require extensive orientation to the imbedded knowledge in the culture. The candidate needs to acquire all the core competencies required of members and leaders up and down the line of the organization in order to appropriately manage the culture.

Threats to the Success of a New Leader

Although the risks we have mentioned may result in the failure to choose an optimal candidate, a transition threat is experienced throughout the entire organization. The primary transition threat in a replication culture is confusion. Because clarity is paramount in these cultures, confusion violates a core value and threatens to destabilize the work.

If a candidate recruited to lead a church has not had adequate grounding in the knowledge embedded in the culture, then he or she may use words or concepts in a way that is significantly unfamiliar for the culture. This ambiguity may be easily tolerated in a family culture where the emphasis is on the relationship, but it can create significant dissonance in a replication culture. The best analogy for this is a replication error in the DNA of a living organism. The reproductive machinery of life makes a great effort to eliminate errors in replicating DNA because so much is at stake in that process. If an error does creep in, it creates a mutant form that competes with the main organism for dominance. Within a replication organizational culture, this constitutes a genuine threat to the future vitality of the church. This is the primary reason that the task of managing transfer of knowledge to the arriving pastor is so critical to the success of the transition.

The shadow transition threat in a replication culture is personal attachment. This is because replication cultures tend to value knowledge and effectiveness in a leader and devalue the personal qualities of the leader that members of the organization attach to. Remember, replication cultures tend to penalize dependency and paternalism and person-centered leadership patterns. This threatens to become a shadow within the organization that members want to avoid or deny.

The issue of personal attachment to a departing leader might not be a significant problem in a replication culture were it not for the fact that members are ashamed or afraid of it. If members do not face this shadow directly, it can emerge as a pseudorational concern around other issues when, in fact, members are simply grieving the loss of a relationship to the previous leader. If helped to acknowledge this shadow, the threat is greatly reduced or eliminated.

Transition Strategies

Pastoral transition strategies in a replication culture are difficult to isolate from the broader succession processes within the congregation. A replication culture church that does not do succession planning well up and down the line is unlikely to be effective in an internal transition at the top. Pastoral transition strategies in replication cultures arise out of general leadership development processes that the church has mastered:

- A clearly articulated philosophy or theology of leadership that is shared throughout the church

- A sophisticated grasp of adult learning principles and the capacity to apply them in training

- Willingness to make significant investment in local educational and training resources

- A non-elitist, flat, organizational structure with a front-line emphasis on facilitating leadership development and deployment

- A growing number of adherents that can serve as a candidate pool for people with high leadership aptitude

- Clear understanding of the leadership roles at various levels of the organization and the ability to do level-appropriate training

- A succession process that builds bench strength at each level of leadership and effectively manages the transition from one leader to another

- A church governance structure that permits internal recruitment to senior leadership levels within the church

- A significant time horizon for development of leaders to senior leadership positions in the church, enabled by the long-term commitment of current leaders

- The capacity of current leaders to mentor and coach successors

- Opportunities for leadership candidates to try on various leadership roles in an exploratory fashion as part of the discernment process

- Feedback mechanisms that give accurate information to leadership candidates to facilitate growth and discernment

- A congregational culture that has "followship resiliency" and can tolerate changes in leadership status among members

- Leadership "hardiness" that can thrive while running counter to the current religious culture tending to be archival, family, or iconic

Advance Planning

Because of the amount of information that must be transferred to a new leader and the need for long-term testing of potential leaders in the current organization, it can require years of preparation to make a leader transition in this culture. If the leader is developed and recruited internally, the transition may require formal seminary education along with more informal educational processes involving mentoring, spiritual direction, workshops, and field work.

In a replication culture where the new leader is recruited externally, much of the training and testing of the candidate takes place in previous positions of leadership. However, planning the transition and the transfer of embedded knowledge in the culture to the new leader and implementing that change can take several years.

Again, it needs to be stated that this is a health-based transition. It assumes that all the key players, including the departing and arriving pastors, are psychologically healthy enough to set aside their egos for the sake of the organization and ultimately the Kingdom of God. Many people argue that it is impossible for the kind of mentoring described in this chapter to take place between a departing and arriving leader. This transition strategy may present difficult and even insurmountable obstacles in other church cultures, but a replication culture may find it desirable. The reality is that many secular businesses have a period of overlap between departing and arriving CEOs for a prescribed period of time and a clearly defined set of tasks. If the governing board is clear about its purposes and if an independent transition consultant is hired to help manage the process (if necessary), there is no reason that a replication church culture cannot successfully navigate a leadership transition and move into the future with strength and vitality.

How It Could Be

Compass Fellowship is a contemporary church begun about thirty years ago by a young college student who believed that people could be reached effectively for Christ in a nontraditional, nonthreatening setting. As it was designed to reach the unbeliever, the emphasis was more on an academic approach than a worship approach. Compass was located in a college community (it has since relocated), and it has caught the interest of students. From the beginning, lives were being changed as a result of this unique ministry.

As the years progressed, the young man finished his education and became a theologian. The Fellowship had grown from a full house to a full warehouse as it reached out to the young nontraditional culture in the area. Musicians were hired to perform religious music of the day, sometimes taking a standard hymn and changing the rhythm, adding instruments and a female singer. Same song, same message, different sound. The time of teaching was passed around among a handful of lead teachers. Gradually, as people married and began families, a Sunday School was formed. Midweek home meetings were established as a way of discipling people.

The Fellowship continued to grow, and eventually it moved to a new campus that would house all of the various ministries being offered as well as provide a facility for conferences and seminars that would attract people from all over the country.

The pastor was nearing age fifty and wondered how much longer he would be able to relate to the younger generation that was pouring through the doors week after week. He began to talk with his church board about the future, and together they decided to seek God's will in determining the direction of Compass Fellowship. It was determined that if there were to be a change in the pastoral leadership it would be filled by someone actively involved in serving the congregation. With no urgency to make a change, the pastor and the board took their time in developing a transition plan that fit their unique ministry. They worked on the plan for months until they had something they believed would work.

They identified the five key players (departing pastor, church board, transition consultant, personnel committee, and arriving pastor) and began the process of moving into a transition by raising up one of the leaders of the Fellowship who had come to faith under this ministry, had been discipled, went on to complete seminary, assumed key leadership and teaching roles, and was ready to take the next step. The pastor mentored this leader, and when the time was right he stepped aside and the new pastor moved into the lead role to take the church forward. It was a smooth transition, because it was well planned not rushed, and about the greater good of the Fellowship instead of egos.

Exhibit 8.1.

Transition at a Glance: Replication Culture

Features

- Leadership traits can be developed rather than simply inherited.
- Leadership knowledge (broad definition) can be transferred from one leader to another.

Language

- Vocabulary varies, but might include equipping, mentoring, coaching, reproducible, discipling, raising up, bench strength, leadership DNA, best practices, training, skill development, benchmarking, "teach a man to fish" and teaching "as you walk on the way" (as well as "I do, you watch; we do, you do; I watch, you do"), capacity building, core competencies, and organizational maturity.

Values

- The values of a replication culture tend to reward standardized content and instructional methods, being teachable and trainable, levels of mastery, having followers, depth and bench strength, clarity, and internal recruitment.
- The values of a replication culture tend to penalize or are passive toward a "star mentality," human-centered leadership, dependency and paternalism, external recruitment of leadership, ambiguity (difficulty in communication and replication), and tradition.

Transition Advantages

- Significant leadership transition experience at other levels of the organization.
- Solid leadership pool that stabilizes the congregation during times of upper-level transition and becomes a source for future leaders.
- Promotion from within means leaders are known, reducing risk of surprises.
- Focus on effectiveness reduces the role of personality as a transitional issue.

Transition Strategies

- A clearly articulated philosophy and theology of leadership that is shared throughout the church
- A sophisticated grasp of adult learning principles and the capacity to apply them in training
- Willingness to make a significant investment in local educational and training resources
- A non-elitist, flat, organizational structure with a front-line emphasis on facilitating leadership development and deployment
- A growing number of adherents who can serve as a candidate pool for people with high leadership aptitude
- Clear understanding of the leadership roles at various levels of the organization and the ability to do level-appropriate training
- A succession process that builds bench strength at each level of leadership and effectively manages the transition from one leader to another
- A church governance structure that permits internal recruitment to senior leadership levels within the church
- A significant time horizon for development of leaders to senior leadership positions in the church enabled by the long-term commitment of current leaders
- The capacity of current leaders to mentor and coach successors
- Opportunities for leadership candidates to try on various leadership roles in an exploratory fashion as part of the discernment process
- Feedback mechanisms that give accurate information to leadership candidates to facilitate growth and discernment
- A congregational culture that has "followship resiliency" and can tolerate changes in leadership status among members
- Leadership "hardiness" that can thrive while running counter to the current religious culture tending to be archival, family, or iconic

Advance Planning

- Long-term advance planning is required for developing senior-level leaders.
- Externally recruited leaders require significant time for enculturation.

Part Three

Components of a Transition Plan

Chapter Nine

Strategic Planning and the Search Process

Any enterprise is built by wise planning, becomes
strong through common sense, and profits
wonderfully by keeping abreast of the facts.
—*Proverbs 24:3–4 (LB)*

Strategic thinking is the conscious, comprehensive, and coordinated decision making of a church to create a future that is significantly different from the present. A *conscious* process is one that forms a vision of the future in the mind that is then created in reality. A *comprehensive* process is one that embraces every element of the church and requires its participation. A *coordinated* effort is one that synchronizes the actions of the elements and capitalizes upon the synergy created by diverse players in common cause so that all ministries achieve a higher level of effectiveness.

The elements of this definition are important. Many churches experience significant changes that can be attributed to positive or negative shifts in their environment. We know that the strongest factor in church growth is numerical growth in the surrounding community. Churches that are well positioned in expanding communities tend to grow without conscious planning. Other churches may have a strong program area that develops under a gifted leader and becomes central to the self-identity of the church. However the effort is neither comprehensive across the entire church nor coordinated. By a combination of the right (serendipitous) circumstances, a church can develop growing and effective ministries without being strategic.

Resistance to Planning Strategically

Many churches resist strategic planning and rely on this serendipity because it seems to exhibit a high level of spirituality. Unfortunately, the results are like the nursery rhyme, "When it is good, it is very, very good. But when it is bad, it is horrid." Cities are littered with closed or closing churches that did not take stock of changes in an environment that eventually proved to be their demise. There is nothing spiritually inferior about a church that discerns a future through the leading of God and moves deliberately toward that future. In fact, one might assume that the ability to discern a future is spiritually preferable. Many churches have learned the painful lesson that to the blind, all is sudden.

A second reason churches may resist strategic thinking is that they understand themselves primarily from a maintenance perspective. The cyclic nature of church life, with repeating weekly experiences encompassed in a larger annual cycle of repeating holidays and seasons, fosters a sense of continuity and order in life. In a world where the rate of change is ratcheting up to ever higher levels, maintenance of continuity and order may be an adequate mission for many churches. Also, when it is perceived that the environment is moving backward spiritually or ethically, an institution that can hold its ground understands itself as successful. In such an organization, those who can effectively operate the ecclesiastical machine and maintain important traditions will be honored above those who catalyze resources to move strategically to a different future. Indeed, catalysts may be pressured to leave.

Maintaining What Is

The first decision before a church is whether to think of itself primarily from a strategic or a maintenance perspective. This requires fearless and honest self-reflection on behalf of leaders and members alike. Maintenance cultures dictate both the kind of pastor who can be successful and the nature of the transition that will be effective. Churches that understand themselves from a maintenance perspective need to have a pastoral transition plan with certain elements:

- Specifications for a candidate who values continuity over innovation, security over risk, and past over future
- Identification of critical maintenance functions and programs that are essential to the success of the church
- A bridging resource that maintains familiar functions and programs
- An orientation process that minimizes change by transferring critical information regarding traditions from the previous pastor to the candidate

Organizational culture may be invisible to the people who live in it, just as air is invisible to us. However, it is the set of ideas, words, values, rewards, and penalties that members of the community breathe every day. Churches need to assess their culture as a way of determining which strategies are effective and which are not.

The community in which I live is ringed with rapidly growing suburban populations. However, many of the mainline denominational churches in these communities are small and plateaued. One does not have to search far for the reasons. These congregations are maintenance cultures, generally of the family type. As we saw in Chapter Five, the values of a family culture tend to penalize (or are passive toward) an emphasis on effectiveness, strategic thinking, discontinuous change, methods, formal processes, experts, credentials, measuring, benchmarking, and outsiders. They do not grow because the culture penalizes activities that may lead to growth. This is not a criticism of any particular church culture; it is a call to radical self-awareness of one's organizational culture, of the power of that culture, and the impact the culture has on pastoral transition.

Charting the Right Course

Almost all the suburban churches just mentioned have gone through a pastoral transition in the last ten years, several more than once. In each case, the new pastor had a limited impact because it is extremely difficult to change organizational cultures. In fact, it is much more likely that a culture will change the leader than that the leader will change the culture. Again, a church must have an accurate understanding of its organizational culture if it is going to be successful in any strategic planning process and pastoral transition. *If the strategic plan runs counter to the organizational culture, the culture will win every time regardless of what the plan says.* This is the reason this book has gone to such great lengths to define churches in terms of cultures and the kind of transition they require.

Here is an analogy. When we plan a trip to visit a certain location by car, we can only arrive if roads have been built that go there. Roads reward people who drive their cars on them. They offer a smooth ride, fuel stops along the way, and signs indicating direction. On the other hand, if you try to travel to a location that has no roads you receive numerous and severe penalties for the attempt. Sharp stones puncture your tires, rough terrain destroys your suspension and exhaust system, trees appear in your way and make forward progress impossible, and your wheels spin uselessly in streams and ponds. You may have a clearly articulated plan to visit a beautiful section of Montana by car, but without roads you will be punished every foot of the way in your attempt.

A strategic plan defines where a church believes it is called to go; a culture is the set of roads (or lack of them) required to go there. Culture defines whether you will be rewarded or punished if you try to get there. Pastoral candidates who are given strategic plans emphasizing the need for growth in a congregation must also discover whether the culture will allow the church to really move in a growth direction.

One church had fifty members when it called a new pastor with the strategic marching orders to grow the church. Fortunately, the church grew. However, many people began leaving the church as it grew. They no longer knew everyone in the church. They believed that people should not be driving a long distance to attend their church when there were other churches closer to home. Multiple worship services split the family and some members stopped coming because they missed seeing everyone at one time. The strategic plan ran counter to the culture.

Using a more technical analogy, culture is like the operating system of a computer—PC or Mac, for example. The operating system defines the kinds of programs you can actually run on the computer. You can have a shelf full of crackerjack computer programs, but they are useless if they are not compatible with the basic operating system of the computer. If you try to run a good program on a poorly matched operating system, you will be penalized every step of the way with error messages and system aborts. One of the most important questions a church must ask is whether a given strategic plan is actually compatible with the organizational culture. For example, a church that sets a strategic target to be diverse will not succeed if it has a culture that penalizes difference of opinion among its members by setting up win-lose scenarios, by marginalizing those who think differently, or by threatening withdrawal if a certain view does not prevail. This is why understanding culture is preliminary to effective strategic planning.

The capacity to think and act strategically is itself an aspect of culture because it assumes that movement, growth, and change are positive. If strategic thinking is consistent with a church's culture, the issue of a pastoral transition must be addressed in a strategic plan. If we define a strategic decision as one that cannot easily be reversed, then choosing a new leader must be counted among the most significant strategic decisions a church will ever make (second only to relocation, addition, or renovation of space). A poor choice of a pastoral candidate or mismanagement of the transition will have long-term and nearly irreversible consequences in the near future. Most churches do not function strategically; those that do function strategically rarely include the pastoral transition as an element of their strategic plan. Our estimate is that less than 1 percent of all churches operate by a strategic plan that includes the pastoral transition as an element of the plan.

Can a Culture Change?

One question that may be floating around in the reader's mind is whether a culture can change. The answer is a qualified yes. The conditions under which a cultural change is possible are rather limited and entail several considerations. First, almost all cultural changes are top down. The executive leader at the head of the organization must take the initiative to articulate a new set of ideas, language, values, rewards, and penalties. Well-intentioned, committed members in the lower ranks of an organization cannot change a culture.

Second, cultural changes can occur during a period of vitality and growth as a natural reaction to change in organizational scale. As a church grows from having twenty-five people in worship to having two hundred, the culture changes from an intimate family culture to a more democratic one. Under the metamorphic pressures of large-scale growth, a family culture church is likely to become an icon culture. However, vitality and growth do not fully insulate an organization from the painful dimensions of cultural change. There are likely to be seasons of power struggle and upheaval, with some members leaving because the social contract has changed. Again, it is the leader who has to bear most of the burden for the transformation.

Cultural changes can occur as the result of a "burning platform." This notion gets its name from a fire on an oil rig in which only the people who took the risk of a jump into the ocean sur-vived. Those who chose to hold onto familiar surroundings per-ished. When a church is facing do-or-die issues, it is sometimes an impetus for cultural change. The key here is whether there is a critical mass of those who (1) take the leap into what is differ-ent and follow a leader in a new direction (unfortunately, in most churches, as was the case on the oil rig, many choose a familiar demise over a risky revitalization) and (2) believe that movement within a given culture is possible with the right leadership and change management. This enables church leaders to make adjust-ments in anticipation of a pastoral transition that lies several years in the future. For example, the vulnerability of an icon cul-ture can be reduced by movement toward replication culture so that there is increased bench strength in the church's leadership. Again, this requires leadership from the top and a clear commit-ment to the church beyond the current pastor's tenure. If it isn't discussed and planned, it won't happen.

Elements of a Strategic Planning Process

If a pastoral transition is a strategic issue, it might be helpful to review the standard elements of a strategic planning process, with a particular focus on the pastoral transition.

Environmental Scan

The purpose of an environmental scan is to familiarize decision makers with characteristics and trends in the environment that may affect the mission of the organization. Demographic changes in a community have a direct and obvious impact on the mission of a church. Less obvious and more difficult to assess are changes in attitudes about organized religion, brand loyalty, and time pressures.

An environmental scan should also include assessment of the pastoral leadership pool. It is important for a church to know:

- The number of possible candidates now and in five-year and ten-year projections. The present lower ordination rates mean a drop in the number of experienced pastors in the future.
- The quality of the candidate pool. Lower scores on ordination exams now, or the lack of successful life experience in other fields among graduates, may mean a smaller number of qualified pastors to assume major leadership roles in the future.
- The level of competition among churches of a given size for leadership. A growing number of large and megachurches with a smaller number of qualified candidates increases competition. This affects pay scales, the time required for a search process, and the necessity for additional training of younger and less experienced candidates.

In general, we live in an environment of significant leadership shortages in both secular and religious institutions. Consider these trends:

- In 2003, the Presbyterian Church had 1,602 churches trying to hire pastors and 1,290 ministers looking for jobs.
- A large number of pastors are now leaving the ministry because they retire or because they quit.
- In the Methodist Church, the number of people entering the ministry between 1981 and 2000 has decreased by 39 percent.
- Twenty-seven percent of U.S. Roman Catholic parishes do not have a priest.
- Churches large and small often have to wait two to three years to find a pastor or associate pastor.

Churches that do not include this kind information in their environmental scan risk inadequate retention efforts on the part of current leaders, substandard pay and benefits, and an unrealistic picture of the duration and expense of a pastoral transition.

Vision Formulation

A vision is the star that guides the organization into its different future. Vision formulation should take into account the core values of the organization coupled with the environment in which the church is functioning. Core values are generated from a church's theological sources as well as its history and local traditions.

Each vision for a church and church culture requires a different kind of pastoral leadership. A church that envisions itself as a family requires a relational pastor, an equipping church may require a teaching pastor, a community transformational church may require an entrepreneurial and collaborative pastor, and a high-profile media church may require a celebrity pastor. Although the vision statement itself may not refer to the pastor's role, the vision formulation process should document the broad parameters of pastoral leadership required for the vision to be accomplished.

SWOT Analysis (Strengths, Weaknesses, Opportunities, Threats)

Once a vision is formulated, an analysis must be conducted that lays the groundwork for how it is to be realized through a specific organization in a specific environment. This involves a comprehensive look at the strengths and weaknesses of the church relative to the vision and at the opportunities and threats to the vision that exist in the environment.

Transition plans should include a process for evaluating the strengths and weaknesses of the staff of a church with respect to the vision. This enables a church's leadership to:

- Develop training programs to shore up staff members in areas of weakness
- Re-recruit key staff members during transition
- Develop bench strength around high performers

- Develop succession plans for leaders to move up to greater responsibility
- Release poor performers to find work in other areas where they can succeed

Strategic Formulation

A vision statement is not actionable; it must be "chunked" into smaller and smaller pieces that finally lead to specific, accountable activities. The actual structure of a strategic plan is not important to our present purposes. What is critical to good strategic thinking is the ability to build on strengths, shore up (or accept) weaknesses, capitalize on opportunities, and neutralize threats in the environment.

The pastoral leader must have the qualities that enable a church to accomplish these strategic objectives. A listing of these qualities constitutes a set of specifications that should be used by the board and the search consultant in recruiting a new candidate. Linking the search process to strategic thinking has a particular benefit in that it produces a health-based approach to specifying a new leader. By *health-based* we mean that the specifications for a new leader are:

- Linked to a positive vision for the future rather than restoring the past
- Built on the strengths of the church, rather than fixing what is broken
- Intended to move the church to the next level of development rather than reduce the church to a previous level and start over
- Focused on new opportunities in the environment for the vision

It is important to understand how this differs from the illness-based model currently in vogue in many churches and denominations.

Illness-Based Transitions and Bridging Resources

An illness-based model assumes that the successes of the church are so inextricably linked to the departing pastor that many of the most effective ministries of the church either have to be intentionally dismantled or allowed to weaken in preparation for a new pastor who will come and resurrect them using a new style, methodology, or allocation of resources. However, this requires that the church experience a double grief simultaneously: loss of the previous pastor and loss of vital ministries as well. It is this double loss that unnecessarily leaves the church vulnerable and weakened. Unfortunately, this is a self-fulfilling prophecy. We assume churches must lose their vitality, so we design transitional schemes to heal them from the loss of their vitality, which only guarantees that they do indeed lose their vitality. It is like sending a doctor instead of food to a person who is starving. Eventually, she will indeed need a doctor because the malnutrition will make her sick. Poor transition planning starves a church into an illness that was not necessary in the first place.

The other problem with an illness-based model is that it is so focused on the illness it makes assumptions about organizations that we would never make about individuals. All persons grieve when they lose a significant relationship. However, not all individuals who lose a significant relationship simultaneously lose their job. When we treat a church that has lost its pastor as if it must now simultaneously lose the vitality of its ministries, we are setting it up for failure.

Strategic thinking sets a context for formulating a transition plan that catalogues the strengths of a church as capabilities that belong to the congregation. These are islands of health that serve as the foundation for future growth. At the same time, strategic thinking recognizes a pastoral change as a possible threat to the realization of the vision. However, rather than assuming a victim mentality relative to this threat and adjusting to its inevitability, strategic thinking establishes tactical measures to counteract it. An effective transition plan aims at ensuring that vital ministries are kept healthy in the transition. Every part of a transition plan should be measured against this criterion: Does it keep ministries vital during the transition?

The discussion of health-based versus illness-based transition models is pertinent to the expectations of bridging resources, particularly when using an interim pastor. In an illness-based model, it is appropriate that the interim pastor focus on grief reduction; basic maintenance ministries such as worship leadership, pastoral care, and administration; and in some cases a deconstruction of existing ministry forms so that the new pastor is able to reshape a ministry around his or her own particular style. In a health-based model, it is more important that the interim pastor work with the lay leadership to identify unique mission components and assets within the congregation that preserve strengths and retain learnings; prepare the congregation for the next steps in its developmental tasks; and maintain leadership focus on the strategic plan, particularly execution of the transition component of that plan.

Transitional Schematic

Next to providing the specifications for the new pastor, the most important element of the transition plan is specifying the relationship between the departing pastor and the arriving pastor. We call this the transitional schematic. The transitional schematic addresses two issues: timing and relationship.

There are three options relative to timing:

1. *Overlapped.* The new pastor arrives and is on the scene several weeks or months prior to the departure of the former pastor so that both are serving the church for a period of time.

2. *Sequential.* The new pastor arrives almost immediately after the departure of the former pastor.

3. *Delayed.* The new pastor arrives several months after the former pastor departs, leaving a period that is covered by interim leadership.

There are also three options for the relationship between the departing and arriving pastor:

1. *Firewall.* The departing pastor has no transitional work relative to the arriving pastor. A clear and impenetrable boundary is established between the two regimes in order to protect the arriving pastor from the biases, preferences, and undue influence of the departing pastor.

2. *Downloading.* The departing pastor transfers information to the arriving pastor that is critical to the vitality of key ministries. This can include information regarding leaders, failure paths, church culture, operational imperatives, organizational capability and maturity, history, land mines, and unique mission components.

3. *Mentoring.* The departing pastor guides the arriving pastor in the process of assuming his or her role as the new leader of the congregation by offering input, feedback, and counsel.

Churches must choose a transition schematic that best fits their particular situation. As a general rule, a small, less complex church has less critical information that needs to be transferred to a new pastor, and the transfer can often be accomplished through lay leaders. Since a small church cannot afford to have overlap timing and cannot pull off the coordination required for sequential timing, the most common transition schematic for a small church is the firewall or delayed arrival.

A larger, more complex church has more information embedded in the organization that is critical to success. An informal information transfer through laypeople is too slow and inefficient to guarantee that ministries will stay vital in the transition. Also, since there is a shortage of leadership for large churches, building leaders internally or recruiting less-experienced leaders often requires a process of mentoring. As a general rule, a larger church requires more time and a richer relationship between the departing and arriving pastors for a successful transition.

Because it can take several years to execute an effective transition plan, planning it well in advance is vital. The first strategic plan developed after the arrival of a new pastor should include the basic elements of a transition plan. This keeps everyone focused on the long-term strength of the church, and honest about how they want the transition to happen. It provides mutual assurances to both church and pastor that honest and forthright discussion about the transition will not result in punitive or precipitous action from either side but instead transpire in a prescribed and thoughtful way. Subsequent strategic plans can become more elaborate about the pastoral transition process.

It may make sense to introduce and develop pastoral transition planning in several stages.

Step One: Crisis Transition Planning

A crisis transition plan describes how the leadership will deal with the sudden loss of a pastoral leader from death, severe illness, accident, an unanticipated call to a different ministry, or dismissal. This plan can be developed using a no-fault approach. It does not assume that the pastor is thinking about leaving or that the leadership is anticipating his leaving. It simply acknowledges that not all events are within our control (a good theological statement) and that the best we can do in certain situations is to be ready.

Step Two: Generic Transition Planning

A generic transition plan furnishes a vision for the pastoral transition. It includes an explication of the Biblical principles that undergird and inform the plan. It articulates the general elements that the church will want to have in place in anticipation of a pastoral transition. It specifies the general transition strategy that the church would want to use (such as delayed arrival or overlapped), who the key players are, what resources the church will use, and how leaders are going to discuss the issue should the pastor begin thinking in the direction of a pastoral transition.

Step Three: Tactical Transition Planning

A tactical transition plan includes all the elements of the generic plan but adds a timetable with objectives and milestones. It includes a communication plan, a budget, and a staff management plan. It identifies unique mission components, specifies how they will be preserved, and how asset transfer will take place.

By establishing transition planning in these steps, we are scaffolding the learning process. Leaders become comfortable working at one level before being asked to step up to the next level, which is to build on the learning of the previous one. This makes the task of transition planning doable while alleviating anxiety around breaking the taboo.

Chapter Ten

The Asset-Preserving Ministry

Test everything. Hold on to the good.

—*I Thessalonians 5:21 (NIV)*

If nature learned from the past as poorly as pastors
learn from one another, we would all still be slime
on a wet rock.

—*Anonymous*

In the late 1980s I was talking to the pastor of a large church with
a significant healing ministry. He had just spoken at a conference
along with his lay leaders about some remarkable experiences
with their healing ministry. One story concerned the miraculous
healing of a child from a congenital defect. The telling of the
story electrified the conference.

In a private conversation with the pastor that evening, the
mood was anything but electric. The pastor was scheduled to
retire. He was certain that the healing ministry in the church he
served would not endure the pastoral transition. The problem was
not the lack of commitment to healing among his leaders; rather,
it lay in the fact that the larger religious system of which his
church was a part would not know how to deal with this distinct
ministry after he was gone. The system would not be able to support what he had built and might even approach it with an eye
to dismantling it as a part of the letting-go process of the previous pastor. With no one available to provide leadership, organizational entropy would gradually take over and the ministry
would fade into a small group in a bulletin announcement.

The dilemma that many church leaders face today is that standard approaches to ministry are no longer effective. Traditional worship, traditional Sunday school, and traditional mission approaches are shepherding a declining and beleaguered flock. Increasingly, effective ministry must be *customized* and *localized* to the particular opportunities that present themselves. However, the very creativity that generates effective ministry leaves it vulnerable in times of pastoral change. A pastor who is used to running Sunday school out of a box of standard curricula in Topeka will have no idea how to support a multigrade, release-time, midweek dinner/discipleship program of a thousand children in Periwinkle. In fact, the success of the ministry in Periwinkle may depend totally upon factors local to that community: the willingness of schools to release students, the public and school transportation system, the relative safety of the community, the number of homes where both parents are working, and the drive time for parents to work.

Unique Mission Components

We call these customized, localized, effective programs unique mission components. These are programs that:

- Have a track record of effectiveness
- Have been customized or localized for a particular situation
- Are at the core of the church's vision
- Require significant oversight or support from the pastor

Each part of this definition is worth an additional paragraph of explanation.

Track Record of Effectiveness

Unique mission components are demonstrably effective. Effective programs accomplish the objectives established by the church using both quantitative and qualitative measures. They have a proven methodology as well as trained and committed leadership, and they represent good stewardship of resources. Like other organizations, churches are loath to face what is no longer working. Sometimes a new pastor is saddled with a host of ineffective programs that he or she is expected to magically invigorate. Generally, this is a waste of resources and should be avoided.

Customized or Localized for a Particular Situation

Unique mission components have been shaped to fit a particular context. Fifty years ago, universal religious programming could be developed in central offices, shipped parcel post, and used effectively in ten thousand locations. Today, we live in an age of localization and specialization. Effective programs must be customized to address generational differences, regional distinctions (try to find an Ohio State sweatshirt in Michigan!), educational backgrounds, vocational choices, commuter patterns, school programming, weather changes, and vacation schedules. The energy invested in creatively tuning a ministry to fit a local context should not be wasted in a poorly managed transition that encourages the organization to forget what it has learned.

The Core of the Church's Vision

A unique mission component is close to the heart of a church's vision; the impact of its loss would be substantial. The vision is the measuring stick by which all decisions are made regarding allocation of scarce resources. A church that has a vision of community transformation may have a thriving book review club that serves a useful function in the church but is not at the core of the church's vision.

Require Significant Oversight or Support from the Pastor

Unique mission components require the attention and energy of the primary leader. Depending on the size of the church, the resources for overseeing many ministries can be entrusted to other leaders. It is not necessary for the pastor to have an intimate working knowledge of them. In contrast, unique mission components require the direct involvement or substantial support of the pastor for their continued success. For example, the responsibility for a building campaign, fundraising, worship design, or leadership formation cannot be fully delegated. These matters lie within the purview of the primary leader, and the new leader must understand the key elements of effective programs in these areas.

Here are examples of unique mission components:

• A unique ministry that has proven to be effective. This might be a healing ministry, a community revitalization ministry, or a particular mission emphasis.

• A unique community in which the church has proven to be effective. This might be a distinct ethnic community, educational community, or sexual orientation in the community.

• Tenure-bridging financial issues. These are long-term financial commitments that require pastoral attention and skill, such as debt reduction or mission funding.

• Tenure-bridging capital issues. These are long-term facility projects that require pastoral attention and skill, such as a building program, renovation program, or land acquisition program.

• A large staff. A church with a large staff is vulnerable because of its complexity. The pastor must be able to work with two constituencies—the congregation and the staff—each requiring a distinct set of tools. Loss of gifted and motivated staff members during a pastoral transition may set the church back years in its work.

• Advanced capacities related to process or planning that are not always understood by interim leaders, nor lie within their expertise. The church becomes vulnerable during transition because the transitional leader does not know how to operate the system. Some churches today have staffs trained in total quality management. Some church staffs are expert in strategic and operational planning. Some have developed advanced leadership development systems involving coaching, mentoring, and tiered training. Many pastors do not have the skills required to manage these sophisticated systems.

Note that some of these factors are more evident in large churches, but some are found in small and midsize churches as well.

Identifying Unique Mission Components

Unique mission components are significant islands of health and strength that the church wants to sustain during and beyond a leadership transition. The first step in sustaining these programs is identifying them. After identifying the critical strategic issues addressed in Chapter Nine, the second important component for a transition plan is identification of unique mission components. They are best identified in a process that includes both professional and lay leadership. It is desirable for the departing pastor *not* to be a part of this process.

Since transition planning is a new experience for most people, an overall context must be set for participants that helps alleviate anxiety and encourage full engagement. Some program directors may feel threatened by the fact that not all ministries are considered unique and vital. It should be explained to them that other parts of the transition plan (see Chapter Eleven) address how to sustain the vitality of all key ministries. Identifying unique mission components for which the pastor has a primary responsibility reduces the risk of the burden falling inappropriately on other staff members.

Next, terms need to be defined. Members will want help understanding what unique mission components are and how to recognize them. Brainstorming possibilities and using the four criteria just mentioned as a grid to evaluate and prioritize may be useful.

Transfer of Assets

After unique mission components are identified, it is important to discover the critical pieces of information for each component that needs to be transferred to the new pastor, particularly the information held by the departing pastor. These critical pieces of information are called assets. The process of transferring these assets from the departing pastor to the new pastor is critical to the success of the transition process and the continuing effectiveness of critical ministries.

Before moving forward to describe how asset transfer can take place, it is worth taking a few sentences to ponder why the process of asset transfer is not intuitively obvious to most churches. There are two possible answers.

Religious Institutions Override Our Intuitions

In the words of Linda Karlovec, an organizational therapist, "many religious institutions today create a disconnect between the member's intuitive guidance system and the dictates of the organization." This is largely because the organization is still operating using a paradigm that was effective fifty years ago but is no longer functional. This forces members into a mode of thinking that does not match their experience—a direct violation of the first principle of adult learning. People often engage in behaviors in religious environments that they would never accept in the secular world, particularly when it comes to the selection, deployment, and expectations of leadership. This results from their having shut down the best thinking that guides them in every other arena of life and turned themselves over to a process that renders them inexpert and dependent. If people are released from the constraints posed by outmoded policies and encouraged to listen creatively to their own intuitive voice, they can reclaim their peculiar wisdom. Theologically speaking, this is the work of listening to the Holy Spirit.

Times Have Changed

Until recently, most church members could be found in small, family culture churches. In this culture, it is assumed that unique and effective ministries are so connected to the personality of the pastor that they are not durable beyond that pastor's tenure. In a family culture, style is everything. Therefore, the best transitional strategy for such unique ministries is to gently but firmly allow them to unravel. Members are encouraged to grieve their loss of these special ministries as an inevitable part of the healing process. Over time they slowly recede from the corporate memory of the church. This makes it easier for the new pastor to arrive and initiate his or her own style-focused ministry, which will have its season of effectiveness inextricably bound to that particular pastor.

This view of ministry substantially denies the possibility of real leadership development. If leadership is purely a matter of style, there can be no mentoring, coaching, skill development, or best practices. Intuitively, we know there is something wrong with this thinking. We would not begin to assume this position in other professions. For example, we believe that medical knowledge is transferable, that it makes sense for physicians to have mentors and nurses to have preceptors. Although physicians may differ in bedside manner (style), there are transferable medical skills that transcend personality. It would make sense to treat a pastor as a similar combination of style and skill and promote the transfer of critical information and development of certain skill sets as part of the transitional process.

Transferring the Assets

Asset transfer can take place in several ways.

Bridging Resource

The bridging resource is an interim team or person put in place to bridge between the departing pastor and the new pastor. The bridging resource can be an interim pastor, a transition team, and/or a professional consultant. The informational assets are transferred from the departing pastor to the bridging resource and then to the new pastor. The advantage of this approach is that it is simpler than overlap strategies that require careful coordination and sequencing.

Pastor-to-Pastor Debrief

A second possibility is that the asset transfer can take place through a pastor-to-pastor debrief. This is a conversation between the departing pastor and the new pastor. It can happen through a period of shared leadership or in a series of conversations scheduled after the previous pastor has departed and the new pastor has been selected. The advantage is that the transfer of information is direct rather than through a third party and less likely to be skewed or distorted. However it happens, it is important that the conversation take place soon enough after the pastor's departure that the information is still accurate and timely. We recommend a delay of no more than six months. After that period of time, memories fade and the accuracy of information begins to deteriorate. It can be helpful to have a structure for this conversation so that power issues do not arise between the two pastors. A starting point for such a structure is the checklist presented in Exhibit 10.1.

Consultant Services

The services of a consultant can be obtained, someone who both guides the church in identifying the informational assets and structures the transfer process in a one- or two-day meeting with the departing pastor and the arriving one. The advantage of this approach is that it lifts the burden of the agenda from both parties and acts as a resource to negotiate any issues related to confidentiality, control, or biases.

Exhibit 10.1.

Pastor-to-Pastor Debrief Checklist

Pastoral

- ☐ Shut-in list
- ☐ Names of terminally ill
- ☐ Names of bereaved in last twelve months
- ☐ Patterns of pastoral care
- ☐ Unusual expectations of pastor
- ☐ Who is angry at the church?
- ☐ Who is angry at the pastor?
- ☐ Who are important allies?
- ☐ Who can't be trusted?
- ☐ Who has an agenda?
- ☐ Who will keep confidences?
- ☐ Who won't keep confidences?
- ☐ Who is sexually aggressive?
- ☐ Who is in danger of burning out?
- ☐ Who is underused?
- ☐ Who has recently retired?
- ☐ Who are the five most influential persons in the church?

Worship

- ☐ Particular traditions and styles
- ☐ Attendance trends
- ☐ Recent controversies
- ☐ Preaching style
- ☐ Time issues
- ☐ Important traditions
- ☐ Seasonal variations
- ☐ Special services

Program

- ☐ Master list of programs
- ☐ Fundraising approaches
- ☐ Giving patterns and records
- ☐ Adult education program
- ☐ Children's education program
- ☐ Youth program
- ☐ Important new programs that need support
- ☐ Older programs that are important
- ☐ Seasonal traditions

Administrative

- ☐ Board role
- ☐ Committee structure
- ☐ Meeting cycles
- ☐ Annual program calendar
- ☐ Financial trends
- ☐ Financial issues
- ☐ Report formats
- ☐ Facility issues and policies
- ☐ Keys and access issues
- ☐ Alarm system

Personnel

- ☐ Staff structure
- ☐ Job descriptions
- ☐ Evaluation processes
- ☐ Staff meetings and agenda
- ☐ Staff issues
- ☐ Recent hires and terminations
- ☐ Training and coaching
- ☐ Confidentiality

(Continued)

Exhibit 10.1. Continued

Church Climate	Unique Mission Components
☐ How warm are church members to one another? To new people?	☐ Unique ministries?
☐ How is the morale in this church?	☐ Unique community?
☐ How open is this church to change?	☐ Tenure-bridging financial issues?
☐ What are the significant conflicts in the church?	☐ Tenure-bridging capital issues?
☐ How central is faith to members' lives?	☐ Large staff?
☐ How conservative or liberal is this church?	☐ Advanced management capacities?
☐ How diverse is this church theologically, ethnically, and demographically?	**Other**
☐ Where are the landmines?	☐ _____
☐ Who are the saints?	☐ _____
	☐ _____

An illustration may be helpful. First Baptist Church concluded $10 million construction of a new facility two years ago. Within a year, $5 million of the construction will have been paid for when the first three years of pledging have been completed. A new debt reduction campaign must be conducted by the end of the year.

The pastor has moved on to another call and the new pastor has just arrived. This church has a unique mission component that we refer to as tenure-bridging financial issues. There are certain informational assets that the new pastor must have in order to be successful in the debt retirement campaign.

Three years before that, the church developed a transition plan in anticipation of the pastor's departure. The board identified the tenure-bridging financial issue as a unique mission component and hired a consultant to manage the asset transfer from the previous pastor to the new pastor.

The consultant called the previous pastor in advance of a planned one-day meeting to gather preliminary information.

Then in a meeting between the previous pastor and the new pastor that was held off site, the consultant conducted a structured informational exchange through an interview; it yielded this information for the new pastor:

- A history of financial campaigns in the church, the general philosophy and theology of giving that had been preached and communicated to the congregation:

    Pledging versus nonpledging

    Tithing versus percentage giving

    Large gift cultivation versus small gift cultivation

    Wills and bequests programs

    Designated giving versus general giving

    Separate mission giving, and so on

- The campaign consultant who was previously used with an assessment of the consultant's effectiveness
- A ten-year financial picture of the church with giving trends, budget trends, and average percentage of household income given to the church
- Financial controls in place, problems with procedures, audits conducted or not
- The names of leaders who were prime movers in the original construction
- The names of leaders who were opposed to the original construction and the issues that were raised
- The names of leaders who were prime movers in raising money for the initial construction
- The people with significant financial resources and their disposition toward the church
- The people who would be able to help solicit large financial gifts
- The people who might oppose a second financial campaign

In addition, the two pastors agreed to certain actions to help bridge from one pastor to the next:

- They coauthored a letter to key persons to inspire leadership for raising the additional money required to retire the debt.
- The former pastor offered letters of introduction to allies within the congregation urging their support for the new pastor's efforts to retire the debt.
- The former pastor agreed to write a letter to members of the congregation at the time of the next campaign as one piece of the marketing strategy urging members to complete with their new pastor what they had begun with their former pastor.

The meeting was designed by the consultant to have a significant spiritual component with Scripture, prayer, and transition principles as a part of the process. The consultant also brought documentation of the process that was jointly approved by both pastors, with a clear statement regarding confidentiality that was signed in advance of the meeting.

An outline of this process, along with a listing of unique mission components and accompanied by the strategic targets discussed in Chapter Nine should be part of the recruitment and negotiation process with a new pastor and included in the exit process with the previous pastor. To emphasize the importance of this process, both pastors should be compensated for their time and expenses. Candidates should be informed regarding the board's expectations relative to this asset transfer.

By focusing on strategic targets, and by building on what is currently unique and effective in the church, the board takes a major step in the direction of a health-based transition. It gives the new pastor a sense of priorities; it equips him or her with critical information required to be successful and avoid failure; it establishes continuity in crucial, often highly visible ministry areas; and it is an opportunity for pastor and successor to demonstrate their alliance for the good of the church and the Kingdom of God.

Of course, every ministry in the church is significant, and an effective transition plan must be thoughtful about how each can be sustained with excellence across a pastoral transition. We now set about the task of examining a model for building capability and maturity in an organization, which makes all ministries more durable.

Chapter Eleven

A Capability-and-Maturity
Model for Churches

... until we all reach unity in the faith and in the
knowledge of the Son of God and become mature,
attaining to the whole measure of the fullness of
Christ. Then we will no longer be infants, tossed back
and forth by the waves, and blown here and there. . . .
—*Ephesians 4:13–14 (NIV)*

It is generally recognized in our society that we face a leadership
shortage. One author refers to the "war for talent" that is domi-
nating corporate culture. Another speaks of the organizational
dilemma in which success requires effective leadership at the very
time that leadership is in short supply. In the succinct statement
of another writer, there just aren't enough leaders.

Churches are not exempt from this scarcity. It is well known
that archival cultures, epitomized by the Roman Catholic Church,
face a severe shortage of priests. Less publicized is the fact that
family cultures in Presbyterian, Methodist, and Lutheran traditions do not have enough pastors to lead them. Large or mega
icon and replication cultures have reached a level of complexity
and sophistication that exceeds the leadership capabilities of all
but a few individuals. The leadership atmosphere in the church
today is extremely rarified.

With some notable exceptions in replication and icon cultures,
most churches recruit pastoral leadership externally rather than
from among their own ranks. There may be good reasons for this
in terms of reducing incestuous leadership risks and destructive

patterns of competition among leaders in local churches, but it tends to externalize the responsibility for developing leaders. Preparing leaders is seen to be the work of other institutions, such as seminaries or regional bodies. The critical link between congregational life and the preparation of leadership is broken. As a result, seminaries lose touch with the realities of congregational life, and congregations focus on the need for pastoral leadership only at those moments when they are in a search process.

The tendency to focus upon this concern primarily as a pastoral recruitment issue is analogous to trying to get apples without apple trees. Leadership does not develop in isolation from an organizational context, and it does not suddenly appear as the result of a graduate degree. If local congregations have a clear understanding of the role of leadership, commitment to cultivate and foster leadership, a method for developing leadership at every level of the organization, and a set of values that reward and celebrate leadership, then they become a pipeline of leadership for the church in other locations, the church of the future, and the community at large.

Faced with the general leadership shortage in the marketplace, many organizations are returning to a philosophy of internal leadership development and recruitment. Though this emphasis does not preclude the need for external recruitment of leadership talent, it shifts the organization toward a more balanced approach in fulfilling its leadership needs. Even though many churches have policies that preclude internal selection of a pastoral successor, they would be strengthened by a commitment to meet their leadership needs internally wherever possible and to make those leaders available to the broader community.

Leadership and organizational vitality are symbiotic qualities. Good leaders are required for organizations to be vital. Vital organizations tend to birth new leaders. The most talented organization will flounder without good leadership. But even the most gifted leader has limited impact on an organization that is not ready. At its best, the leader-organization relationship is a three-legged race where both are in sync. There is a palpable threshold that is crossed when this begins to happen. Some aspects of this can be captured in performance data for the church: worship attendance, financial giving, member engagement, mission involvement, and so on. Other aspects are less tangible: a feeling of health, a spirit in the air, or a sensation of energy. Theologically speaking, this might be described as the presence of the Holy Spirit.

However it is perceived, when a leader-organization partnership begins to click it is important to capture some of the energy of that marriage to mature and expand the competencies of the organization. This in turn feeds the leadership development effort in a symbiotic process.

The Stewardship of Leadership

Leadership tends to emerge out of organizations that are successful in accomplishing their respective missions. Two concepts are helpful in thinking about the strength of an organization: *capability* and *maturity*. Capability is the capacity of an organization to be effective in what it sets out to do. Maturity is the ability of an organization to take responsibility for the effectiveness of its work rather than assign it to a few people (or only one). Churches may differ in theological perspective, community setting, and size, but there are certain generic processes that are mastered as the organization becomes more capable and mature. Understanding what these generic processes are and recognizing them (or their absence) in a church gives us a way of determining how capable and mature an organization is and what leadership is needed at that stage or to move to a new stage.

It has been said that it is impossible to manage what we cannot measure. If we are going to grow churches that are more capable and mature, we need a way of measuring that capacity. The capability and maturity of the organization or any part of it can be categorized at one of four levels.

Level Zero: Not Performing

A level zero church does not produce an effective ministry in the area under consideration. There may be persons assigned to the task (as in a committee). They might even hold meetings. However, most of the group energy is absorbed in such maintenance functions as tending to differences, debating approaches, seeking resources, or political posturing. Expertise, even in one individual, is lacking or stifled.

If a ministry is produced, it is difficult to access because of schedule, visibility, or facility issues. Or the ministry may not be of sufficient quality to meet the needs or aspirations of the members. Level zero churches should not be engaged in programs of leadership development because they tend to replicate incompetence. Instead, the primary tasks of a level zero church should be:

- Creating awareness of islands of health in the larger church as possible models
- Developing readiness in the organization to be led and taught
- Borrowing leadership from successful organizations by forming partnerships and alliances

Level One: Person-Driven

A level one church produces an effective ministry in the area under consideration. It is generally acknowledged that the ministry is performed as expected or required by those served. However, performance depends on individual knowledge and effort. There may be people assigned to the task (a committee), but it is clear that the effort is successful because of the expertise and commitment of one key person. This leader manages the process through his or her personality or position. The process by which the ministry is performed is implicit in the mind of the leader, and members respond to the leader's direction, often in a command-and-control manner.

Because ministry is produced through a key leader who manages through his or her personality, level one churches produce heroes. Without the hero the ministry is neither repeatable nor reproducible in other persons.

Level one churches are those beginning to click. In the area of effectiveness, they have a leader who is able to manage himself or herself and perhaps manage other people. Some leadership development is possible in this organization, with the primary tasks being:

- Externalizing the vision, knowledge, and values of the effective leader so they can be transmitted
- Growing the effective leader from the role of hero into the role of trainer with the accompanying skills and emotional maturity required in that role
- Developing readiness in the organization to be trained and deployed

Level Two: Team-Driven

A level two church produces an effective ministry in the area under consideration. However, level two churches differ from level one churches in that they produce the ministry in a manner that is planned and tracked by a group of people who all understand how and why the ministry works. The level two ministry is no longer dependent on the knowledge or skills of one key person. An entire team has sufficient understanding of the ministry and control of it to take these measures:

- Determine the resources necessary to provide the ministry (budgets and personnel)
- Assign responsibilities for carrying out the ministry

- Furnish the tools necessary for the ministry
- Provide training for the people actually performing the ministry
- Develop plans, standards, and procedures for how the ministry is being conducted
- Verify compliance with the plans, standards, and procedures
- Measure how well the ministry is being performed
- Make corrections if the ministry is failing to meet expectations

Level two churches have fully crossed the threshold with leaders and organization in sync. In addition to performing the tasks of the ministry, this church should be setting about these additional tasks:

- Developing a succession plan for leadership within their ministry area
- Providing leadership training for other churches
- Identifying candidates for service at a higher level, as a "manager of managers" rather than simply manager of a team

Level Three: Innovation-Driven

Like level two churches, level three churches produce a ministry in a way that is planned and tracked. However, the level three church has a greater understanding of the parameters within the development of the ministry that make it more or less effective. A level three church tends to be more focused on quantitative measures than a level two church. It is more aware of capabilities and how to maximize them. It has enough knowledge of the interface between culture and ministry to know which factors to address in trying to improve effectiveness. It knows the best practices being used today, and it has a surplus of energy that enables them to absorb the risks of innovation and creativity.

To illustrate these levels, let's take the ministry with which we are all probably most familiar: worship.

Worship, Level Zero: Not Performing

Worship fails to meet the expectations, needs, and aspirations of most participants. Worship attendance is declining or reduced to a faithful core, and morale in the church is low.

Worship, Level One: Person-Driven

Worship meets the expectations of most worshipers through one key individual, the pastor.

Worship, Level Two: Team-Driven

Worship meets the expectations of most worshipers through a carefully planned and tracked process involving not only the pastor but also music staff, liturgists, ushers, publicists, printers, technicians, and others. The knowledge required for an effective worship experience resides in the minds of a number of people. Several people in the leadership pool are skilled homilists.

Worship, Level Three: Innovation-Driven

The process includes an awareness of best practices; inclusion of key quantitative information such as the amount of parking needed, sanctuary capacity, child care provisions; and introduction of innovative ways of reaching new people.

Notice that at each higher level, the capability developed within the organization increases. By determining the capability and maturity of a given ministry, decisions can be made regarding goals for further development and the likely impact of a pastoral transition upon that ministry. We offer you a tool in Exhibit 11.1 to assist with this assessment process.

Exhibit 11.1.

Capacity-and-Maturity Tool

If the Ministry:

- Is not occurring regularly
- Does not meet minimal standards for effectiveness
- Is engaging a shrinking number of participants
- Is stagnant in a growing community
- Has low morale
- Experiences recurrent, unresolved conflict

Then the Church Is at
Level Zero, Not Performing

If the Ministry:

- Is occurring regularly
- Is meeting minimal standards for effectiveness
- Has sustained vitality
- Engages a growing number of participants

And Success Is Attributable to a Single Person's

- Presence at the ministry
- Knowledge of how the ministry works
- Directive leadership

Then the Church Is at
Level One, Person-Driven

If the Ministry:

- Is occurring regularly
- Is meeting minimal standards for effectiveness
- Has sustained vitality
- Engages a growing number of participants

And Success Is Attributable to a Group of Persons Who

- Share knowledge of critical success factors
- Are cross-trained (know each other's jobs)
- Provide bench strength (multiple quality leaders at key positions)
- Plan and track the success of ministry

Then the Church Is at
Level Two, Team-Driven

If the Ministry:

- Is occurring regularly
- Is meeting minimal standards for effectiveness
- Has sustained vitality
- Engages a growing number of participants

And Success Is Attributable to a Team of Persons Who

- Have knowledge of best practices of the church today
- Benchmark against other ministries
- Understand quantitative drivers
- Risk creative innovation at changes of scale in the ministry

Then the Church Is at
Level Three, Innovation-Driven

A church comprises its own distinctive set of ministries. Ministries in the life of a church function at different levels. Analysis of each of the functional areas is helpful in understanding the capability and maturity of each area, and the capability and maturity of the organization as a whole. This begins with identifying the key ministries of a church (for example, worship, mission, administration, education, and membership). When analysis of the capability and maturity of each area is conducted, a composite of the church overall can be generated, as in Exhibit 11.2.

Exhibit 11.2.

Composite Analysis: Capability and Maturity

Ministry Area	Current State of Capability-and-Maturity Level	Three-Year Goal for Capability-and-Maturity Level
Preaching	1	2
Music	2	2
Adult education	1	2
Evangelism	0	1
Lay visitation	0	1
Personnel	1	2
Mission	1	2
Youth ministry	2	3
Property	2	2
Children's ministry	1	1
Staff management	1	2
Member care	0	1
Social action	0	1
Fundraising	1	2

Capability at the Time of Transition

What happens when there is a pastoral transition? It depends on the capability of the organization and the transition strategy adopted by the leaders. Let's look at some examples.

Level Zero Transitions

If the church is at level zero (not performing), a pastoral transition cannot hurt the church since it is not functioning at a satisfactory level anyway. In fact, the opposite may be true. A level zero church may benefit from a transition, with an elevation of expectations for the future. However, it is critical in the transition that readiness, awareness, and partnerships be developed in preparation for a new leader. If these tasks are not accomplished, it is unlikely that a new leader will be able to create the synergy needed for renewal (see Chapter Twelve).

Level One Transitions

If the church is at level one (person-driven), the loss of the pastor brings about an acute trauma. The members lose not only a counselor, healer, and friend but also the key to their effectiveness in ministry. To recoup this loss, they look forward to a new pastor who will fulfill all these roles.

In this situation, an appropriate transitional ministry may be grief-focused, helping people process their loss and come to closure. It will also work to loosen up any procedures put in place by the former pastor as preparation for a new pastor who may do things differently. In a level one church, it is assumed that any process or program capacities developed in the congregation are of secondary importance to the capacities brought to the church by the new pastor.

Level Two Transitions

Let's assume the church that has just lost its pastor is at level two (team-driven). What if the transitional ministry uses a level one strategy? The leadership fails to recognize the competency within the congregation to perform this ministry effectively, including the ability to plan and track. They let this capacity lie fallow, which causes it to atrophy. Now members have two losses, first the pastor and then their own sense of power and ability. Because the leadership is using a level one transition strategy, they wrongly interpret this as a grief reaction to the loss of the former pastor alone. They passively encourage dismantling of congregational processes in preparation for the next pastor. What the transitional leadership has unwittingly accomplished is the backward movement of a congregation from level two to level one.

The congregation intuits this loss of capacity and looks for a hero to be the next pastor, consistent with level one. This in turn sets up the next pastor to fail.

Level Three Transitions

In level three (innovation-driven) ministries, the team members are so specialized and expert that their capacity exceeds that of most all generalists, including pastors. This level of capability and maturity can be threatening and confusing to transitional leaders, especially if they are accustomed to a family culture in which the pastor is the resident expert on all matters related to the functioning of the church. If the transitional resource (interim pastor) assumes that the ministry team is merely being recalcitrant, he or she may drive the capability level of the ministry back to previous levels where there is a dependency on the pastor.

The Story of Glendon Community Church

Glendon Community Church had a vision of reaching its community with the transformational message of the Gospel. The church had high expectations for its lay leaders and gave little status per se to ordained positions except within the functions of teaching, preaching, and sacraments. The leadership believed that gifted, committed, and motivated laypeople can perform many traditional pastoral duties as well as ordained clergy. Members were engaged in hospital visitation, prayer for the sick, management, and coaching roles.

Therefore when the church configured its staff it chose a staff heavy in lay professionals and light in ordained clergy. It then offered a significant body of training to both staff and ministry leaders. Staff members were trained in total quality management, with skills in teamwork, collaborative decision making, problem solving, customer service, coaching, strategic planning, listening, confrontation, assertiveness, rational emotive self-management, gift assessment, and personality inventory.

Ministry leaders were given similar training, with more emphasis on strategic thinking, goal and objective development, prayer, and accountability. A churchwide organization of ministry leaders was put in place that met quarterly to set goals, evaluate progress, celebrate victories, learn from mistakes, and receive ongoing training.

In the absence of the pastor, staff members were competent to carry on the work of the church. Staff teams were led by lay professionals, and the acting head of staff was a lay professional as well. Lay ministries proliferated in the church.

This emphasis on the leadership development of the church gave it high bench strength and a high level of capability and maturity. Many ministries were functioning at level two (team-driven), with a whole team possessing the knowledge and skills required to effectively operate their area of ministry. Two were functioning at level three (innovation-driven).

When the pastor left, the church was operating effectively under the leadership of the staff and lay ministers, which had been developed over the years. However, under pressure to adopt a more traditional approach to the transition, the board called a bridging resource, an ordained interim pastor who was not trained in most of these management and leadership skills. He knew the church had been effective but assumed it was effective only because of the gifts and style of the previous pastor (level one). He then proceeded to dismantle the leadership structure that the church had worked five years to build on the grounds that it was a remnant of the previous pastor. What he dismantled was something he had never seen before and could not recognize as an advanced capability—a level two church. When members expressed dismay and frustration that they were not being permitted to function in the full strength of their training and gifts, they were told they needed to let go of the old way of doing things.

If this bridging resource person had been better trained, he would have recognized these level two and level three capacities and sought to conserve them as the building blocks for the next phase of development in the life of the church. Instead, the next pastor inherited a frustrated and disempowered set of leaders who were thrust back into a role of dependency that they had moved past years before. The new pastor also interpreted this frustration as a loss of level one effectiveness connected to the previous pastor and instituted measures to heal the congregation of its grief. This process only deepened the frustration as members felt they were not being heard.

All the costs described in Chapter Two began to accrue. Attendance dropped to a third of its peak. Revenue fell off substantially, creating a problem with debt reduction on the $2 million renovation and expansion that had been completed five years earlier. Staff positions had to be cut and programs slashed. Half of the search committee has now left the church. Today, Glendon Church is a typical one, with a few ministries that are effective primarily when the pastor is there.

Distinct Needs at Every Level

Each level has its own distinct needs during a pastoral transition. At each level, certain things must be grieved, certain things have to be conserved, and certain things should be clarified.

Level Zero Transitional Needs

A level zero church is not producing a viable ministry. Members need to grieve lost opportunities and failures of the past. It is important to conserve relationships among the members as a base for future vitality. The church requires help clarifying what it needs in order to function at the next level (level one, person-driven). This understanding sets the stage for establishing plans for the future, including the work of the next pastor.

Level One Transitional Needs

A level one (person-driven) church has been producing a viable ministry, but much of it is derived from the pastor who managed the church through his or her personality. The loss of the pastor is felt acutely because the church has not only lost its relational center but also its reservoir of skill that is key to the success of the church's programs. In the transition, it must grieve this loss and bring closure. It needs to conserve relationships and the key programs that have been set in motion. It will have to clarify whether it wants to remain a person-driven church or move to being a team-driven church. This has implications for its next pastoral search.

Level Two Transitional Needs

A level two (team-driven) church has been producing a viable ministry through a set of process skills understood and executed by members of the congregation. In a pastoral transition, members grieve the loss of the pastor, as in the previous level. However, because some skills have been retained, the grief need not be as deep as for a person-driven church. These process and ministry skills must be conserved by the interim leadership, who have to be skilled enough to recognize and sustain them. Also, a team-driven church should clarify whether it wants to move to being an innovation-driven church.

Level Three Transitional Needs

A level three (innovation-driven) church has an even greater level of achievement in process and ministry skills, with a broader understanding of qualitative benchmarks. The grief work is reduced, and the conservation work becomes increasingly significant if the church is not to lose ground in the interim period. Clarification needs to focus on particular mission options, not processes for addressing them.

In general, the higher the level of capability and maturity in an organization, the less its life is enmeshed with that of the leader. The role of the leader shifts from father, mother, or sole driver of the organization to guarantor of compliance to processes that maximize the gifts, skills, and expertise of the members and that move the organization forward toward its vision. In higher-level organizations, transitional leadership must invest more of its energy in conserving these processes. This is possible because less energy is required to deal with the loss of the pastor. The level of loss is actually reduced since the pastor no longer takes such a large percentage of the skill set with him or her at departure (Exhibit 11.3).

As churches plan for pastoral transition, it can be helpful for them to assess their level of capability and maturity in the various key ministries they are performing. This requires a significant level of courage and self-awareness. Through clarity on this issue they can better capitalize on their internal leadership and prepare to move forward without inadvertently sabotaging the leadership they have developed over the years. They can also specify for potential pastors where their church is in terms of its capability and maturity as well as where they want the next pastor to take them in the future.

With the analysis of the capability and maturity of the church complete, a church's leadership is now equipped to craft a fully orbed transition plan that takes into account the culture of the church, strategic direction, key players, roles, process, unique mission components, and asset transfer. These components are listed in Exhibit 11.4.

Exhibit 11.3.

Transitional Needs by Capability-and-Maturity Level	
Church Level	*Need During the Transition*
Level zero, not performing	• Need to grieve lost opportunities, past failures • Need to conserve relationships • Need to clarify how to move to level one • Need to prepare for level one
Level one (person-driven) (relationship, skills)	• Need to grieve lost pastor • Need to conserve relationships • Need to clarify whether to move to level two • Need to prepare for level one or two
Level two (team-driven) (relationship, trainer)	• Need to grieve lost pastor • Need to conserve effective leaders, processes, and programs • Need to clarify whether to move to level three • Need to prepare for level two or three
Level three (innovation-driven) (relationship, consultant)	• Need to grieve lost pastor • Need to conserve all those in level two plus quantitative data and benchmarking • Need to clarify whether to stay at level three • Need to prepare for level two or three

Exhibit 11.4.

Comprehensive Transition Plan Components

A description of the church culture:

- Key ideas
- Language used
- Values
- The advantages and challenges of this culture in the transition and how the leadership will address them

A strategic plan that includes:

- A vision for the church
- A vision for the pastoral transition process with guiding spiritual principles
- A description of the pastoral recruitment environment
- A full definition of the transition process, strategies, and key players

A definition of unique mission components along with a process for asset transfer

A description of all the key ministries of the church, their level of maturity, and the leaders' goal regarding future maturity

---

Chapter Twelve

Pastoral Transitions in Low-Performing Churches

> Therefore, strengthen your feeble arms and weak
> knees. "Make level paths for your feet," so that the
> lame may not be disabled, but rather healed.
> —*Hebrews 12:12–13 (NIV)*

An early reviewer of this book posed the question, "What is your message to congregations, the majority of which are unhealthy and dysfunctional?" It is an important question, not only for what it asks but also for what it states. The church context of today is a sea of dysfunctional tendencies, some brought on by the larger society, but many inherent in the church itself.

One of the challenges posed by dysfunctional systems is that, given enough time, they normalize the abnormal behavior that eventually leads to a crisis. It is the familiar frog-in-the-kettle story played out on the corporate level, in which small changes accommodated over time lead to a life-threatening crisis. The problem is that *it doesn't feel like a crisis.* People who are living in dysfunctional religious organizations may not feel that something is wrong. Unfortunately, the converse is also true. When people who have lived in dysfunction for a long time experience health, health feels odd to them. It may even make them angry. Even when health is introduced and experienced, people may slip back to what is less healthy because it is familiar.

As we have heard many times from pulpits, it only took a day to get Israel out of Egypt, but it took forty years to get Egypt out of Israel! For those conditioned to be slaves, freedom can produce an intolerable anxiety. For those who grow up abused, the absence of abuse can produce a gnawing guilt. For those who grow up with low expectations or none, discovering the potential of their lives can produce a kind of panic. As Nelson Mandela said, "Our greatest fear is not that we are inadequate, but that we are powerful beyond measure." Both of us as authors have experienced dysfunction at the personal and organizational levels, and we know firsthand the forces that keep us stuck in an unhealthy place.

But we also know that the way out is through. Through the discomfort. Through the awkwardness. Through the conflict and chaos.

If you sense that we have primarily addressed pastoral transition for healthy congregations, you are right. Our reason for this focus is not a lack of compassion for those who are struggling. By doing so, we are walking our talk. Just as we believe that the renewal of individual congregations requires an internal focus on islands of health, we also believe that the renewal of the Christian church in North America requires a focus on congregations that have discovered how to be strong and resilient. Effective pastoral transitions are one critical component of that renewal.

What happens to those congregations that are not healthy? The full answer to that question lies well beyond the scope of this book. But our recommendations to struggling congregations regarding pastoral transition require a partial answer and a bigger picture that we now paint in broad strokes.

Though we used the word *dysfunctional*, we would now like to jettison it for a more precise vocabulary that we have already introduced. As we look at all the churches in North America, we see that most of the congregations lack capability and maturity. They are ineffectual in performing functions that are critical to their success (lack of capability), and what capability they have is dependent upon one or two key individuals (lack of maturity). We refer to these as low-performance churches (for an example, see Chapter Eleven).

We caution you not to assume that low-performance churches are primarily small. Large churches that have been plateaued for a number of years in worship attendance, financial giving, and educational programs or that have begun to decline may be moving into the low-performing category. Larger churches may have the resources that enable them to work around their low performance in the short run. The problem for smaller churches is that they do not have this luxury. For these churches, low performance means a survival crisis.

In the midst of the low-performance churches we are describing, there are congregations that are islands of health. They have learned how to be effective in performing critical ministries, and they have learned how to reproduce leadership for these effective ministries so that they have bench strength and resilience. These islands of health can be found in a variety of contexts: urban, suburban, small town, rural. They can be found in all sizes: small, medium, large, mega. What they share is that they have learned as organizations how to be effective and mature.

It is in the interest of the Church in North America, regardless of denominational, nondenominational, or interdenominational commitments, that these congregations find a way to protect their health and retain their learnings as a resource for us all. The current model of pastoral transition, left over from a time when organizational learning was not as important, does not help congregations protect what is healthy and retain what they have learned. It is the organizational equivalent of burning down the community library every time a new mayor is elected, as if the only information we now need is what the latest mayor brings.

Systems that focus on fixing what is broken soon discover that they do not have enough resources and that they are cannibalizing what is healthy just to stay alive. In systems that learn from discovering their healthy components and that nurture them, the system tends to be self-healing.

Two system analogies might be helpful. The first is a medical analogy. A growing body of research indicates that the immune system is strengthened by positive, meaningful life experiences. This is an issue of perception; what is positive and meaningful varies from person to person. If the person experiences life as positive and meaningful—whatever the experiences—the immune system is strengthened.

Another body of research indicates that cancer cells form with regularity in the body. However, if the immune system is robust, they are destroyed before they get a foothold.

The classic treatment of cancer involves fixing what is broken using surgery, chemotherapy, and radiation. In many cases, there are inadequate resources to fix the problems, the cancer overwhelms the patient, and the patient dies.

However, one body of research has shown that half of terminally ill cancer patients go into long-term remission if they are helped to recover the dream for their lives that they gave up and *begin to act upon it*. For reasons not fully understood, concrete steps taken in the direction of recovering a lost dream in a person's life trigger a resurgence in the immune system that is often strong enough for the body to heal itself when surgery, radiation, and chemotherapy have not been effective.

The church's focus on fixing what is broken (surgery, radiation, chemotherapy) and its benign neglect of what is strong and healthy (ask any pastor of an effective ministry how many times denominational officials have called and asked how they can learn from and expand their health and strength) is preventing the system from learning and healing itself.

A second analogy has to do with youth ministry. A growing body of research indicates that protective factors in the lives of children are more powerful than risk factors. This means that a single adult in the life of a child who takes a personal interest in the child and envisions the child's greater possibilities can outweigh a number of environmental risk factors such as poverty or drugs and alcohol. In other words, society is better served if we invest our resources in developing protective factors rather than trying to eliminate all the risk factors. In fact, a focus on the risk factors can actually have a detrimental effect as it gives a child the impression that he or she is destined to fail because of them.

There are a number of risk factors in the corporate lives of churches today: a hostile culture, declining membership and financial resources, aging facilities, shifting populations. What we are learning, though, is that a focus on these risk factors may be counterproductive. Treating churches as if they are sick only increases their tendency toward pathology. Turning the attention of churches to protective factors and to building on islands of health is more promising to our future.

Specifically, how can this happen?

Focus on Best Practices

Best practices are the methods of ministry that have a proven track record of effectiveness for a given context and are reproducible on the part of a variety of leaders. Discovering these best practices, training members in them, and implementing them locally is critical to the renewal of a low-performance church. By way of contrast, low-performance churches tend to engage in zero-based program development. Rather than learning what has been effective in other similar contexts, they start from scratch. We would never go to a heart surgeon who learned surgery this way! Why do we think we can develop ministries to souls like this? The result can be a well-intentioned pooling of ignorance that leads to what has always been done before.

Develop Patching Strategies

In the old days, when tires had inner tubes, patches were placed on the outside to connect one part of the rubber to another part of the rubber and bridge across a hole. Today we need strategic patches that connect leaders to leaders informally so that learning can take place, particularly around the issues of best practices. The reason a patch is a good analogy is that it is an addition to the system that is applied at the surface. Centrally controlled communication structures found in denominations are too rigid and unresponsive to serve as communication channels for best practices. By the time the information is acquired, debated as to orthodoxy, scrutinized as to political impact, written, published, and distributed . . . the environment has changed and the information is out of date. What is needed is a patch that connects frontline leader to frontline leader at the surface of ministry, regardless of denominational affiliation. This connection can take place through conferences, workshops, journals, personal conversations, e-mails, and websites.

Emphasize Organizational Learning and Development

Organizations learn, grow, and develop much as individuals do. It is important to understand that this process is not linear. Organizations grow by encountering crisis, accompanied by temporary regression to a less mature state, but with the right supports (material resources, expertise, and love) they can then develop to a higher level. Organizations that understand this process, that take a positive perspective on what is happening, that are committed to learning and growth and to retaining the learnings they have achieved, and that take the initiative to find the resources they need at those critical moments can thrive through crisis. The resources they need are often found by way of other leaders who have been effective in similar contexts . . . the islands of health.

Leaders and Creating Change in Culture

For churches to be effective, a change in the culture is usually required: the central ideas, the language used, the values adopted, and the rewards and penalties that support them. Cultural change is almost always top-down. It is a leadership task that cannot be delegated. Inevitably, cultural changes in an organization result in a period of conflict and some loss. This means that the leader must be emotionally and spiritually hardy. Here we mean that the leader is resilient in the face of setbacks and can "take a licking and keep on ticking." Resilience is developed when the leader has a number of assets, including spiritual resources, exercise, recreation, health, hobbies, financial stability, friendship, and adequate support inside and outside the organization. The islands of health can be key support components for such a leader.

Implement Adult Learning Strategies

Adults do not learn in the same way as children do. Adults need to be participative in their own learning process; they need bridging strategies that connect what they already know to new information and they need immediate opportunities to apply what they have learned.

We know that adults remember only 10 percent of what they hear but 90 percent of what they hear, say, and do. We also know that in an emotionally charged situation, people revert not to what they have learned but to what they have practiced. Preaching as the only source of instruction does not help the organization learn fast enough. There must be opportunities for participation, practice, and application. It is essential to have connections to other parts of the Body of Christ where people have learned what is effective and are doing it. This can happen through workshops and practicums led by those who have a proven track record and who are giving hands-on training rather than using cognitive and didactic approaches alone.

Focusing on islands of health is not dismissive to low-performance churches. It is, given the right connecting strategies, the ultimate hope for them. By building on the health within the system and creating effective, surface-level, frontline connections, we believe the system can eventually heal itself.

What are the implications for pastoral transitions in churches that have low capability and maturity?

First, *use the transitional moment as an opportunity to precipitate a crisis that can make change possible.*

It is generally the case that a church is headed toward crisis long before it is in crisis. This means that a governing body with oversight responsibilities and the means of monitoring the health of the church can intervene at an early stage of declining performance with the hope of change. It can extrapolate recent trends and the broader experience of the church to show that change is required. Nonperforming, immature churches have lived in their current state for so long that ineffectiveness has come to feel normal to them. Unless a crisis is created around their current state, there is neither pain enough nor hope enough to motivate change. The pastoral transition can create the opportunity for an intervention that precipitates this crisis.

Second, *interview candidates*.

Choosing the right leadership for a low-performance church is critical. Here the issue is less one of how to sustain what is currently effective and more a question of whether the candidate can bring an infusion of information regarding effective ministry models. Interviewing bodies should consider the inquiries made of candidates:

- Discover their knowledge of best practices in six critical areas:
  Worship
  Adult learning
  Youth ministry
  Fundraising
  Mission
  Evangelism
- Explore their own patching strategies:
  Do they have a mentor? Was the mentor successful?
  Are they networked to other successful ministries in a similar context to yours? What is the network?
  What are their information sources for building capability within a congregation?

- Explore how they would handle a developmental crisis within the church:

  Do they understand what a developmental crisis looks like (adding a second worship service, for example)?

  What external resources would they bring to the church to help it through a change process?

  What expertise do they have related to organizational change?

- Explore their understanding of culture change and conflict:

  Which ideas, vocabulary, and values are critical for the church to be effective today?

  How would they reward and recognize the right values, and penalize or ignore the less desired ones?

  How will they find support during a time of conflict?

  How emotionally and spiritually resilient and hardy are the candidates?

- Explore their understanding of how adults learn:

  What are the key components of adult learning?

  What are the key adult learnings required of members in an effective church?

  How would they go about implementing an adult learning strategy in the church?

Develop Critical Mass

For change to take place, there must be a competent leader, a majority of people who will give permission, and a critical mass of people who can model the future. This critical mass may represent as little as 20 percent of the congregation, but they can articulate a different future, offer leadership to key ministries, provide substantial financial backing to the work of the church, and support the pastor in the change process. This support should be formalized in the negotiations to call a new pastor.

Strategies for pastoral transition in a struggling church are simultaneously less complex and more difficult than in strong congregations. Because there are fewer components of health to carry across the transition, bridging strategies can be simplified and asset transfer is less an issue. However, selecting, preparing, and supporting a leader for this task requires more awareness and a greater commitment on the part of congregation if the transition is to be successful.

Exhibit 12.1.

Transition Strategies for Low-Performance Churches

Use the transitional moment as an opportunity to precipitate a crisis that can make change possible.

Interviewing candidates:

- Discover their knowledge of best practices in five critical areas:
    Worship
    Adult learning
    Youth ministry
    Fundraising
    Mission
- Explore their own patching strategies
- Explore how they would handle a developmental crisis within the church
- Explore their understanding of culture change and conflict
- Explore their understanding of how adults learn

Develop critical mass:

- At least 20 percent of the congregation
- Can articulate a different future
- Offer leadership to key ministries
- Provide substantial financial backing
- Support the pastor in the change

Chapter Thirteen

A Plan for Responding to the Crisis of Sudden Transitions

> Now listen, you who say, "Today or tomorrow we
> will go to this or that city, spend a year there, carry
> on business and make money." Why, you do not
> even know what will happen tomorrow.
> —*James 4:13–14 (NIV)*

Church folks would be the first to admit that ultimately only God is in control. Unexpected events happen to all of us, and humility requires us to acknowledge our frailty in the face of forces larger than ourselves. Yet church leaders often operate without the slightest idea of what they will do if their pastor is suddenly taken from them.

We cope with the unexpected by devising crisis and contingency plans. Every time we get into a car and snap a seatbelt around our waist, we are establishing a crisis plan. We are not in control of every other driver on the road, let alone large animals, weather, landslides, earthquakes, pedestrians, or mechanical failure in our vehicle or someone else's. Nor are we fully in control of ourselves, sudden distractions, health emergencies, or people within our vehicle. A seat belt is a crisis plan that says, "If something unexpected happens and this car hits a large object, I have a plan for protecting my body from severe injury."

It is sobering to realize that most churches do not have a plan in place that will manage the risk of a sudden pastoral departure. The reasons why a pastor might suddenly leave generate a substantial list:

- Sudden onset of a debilitating physical illness
- Mental illness, emotional collapse
- Traumatic event in the life of a family member
- Death by accident, catastrophic health problem, or violence
- Family problem such as divorce
- Personal problems that necessitate dismissal
- An unexpected, but desirable ministry opportunity for the pastor, with a short time line

Some of these events are more likely than others and all are things we would rather not think about; nevertheless, real-life examples come to mind in every case. Taken together, the possibility of a sudden pastoral departure is real and worthy of attention.

Elements of a Crisis Plan

The critical elements of any crisis plan are safety, command structure, continuity of service, communication, and restoration of normalcy. When a pastor departs suddenly, each is an issue; a crisis plan should address them all.

Safety

The plan should provide a way to ensure the physical, emotional, and spiritual safety of members. If the pastor has died suddenly, critical incident debriefing may be necessary for the church staff and lay leadership, and perhaps for the entire church. Since the sudden death of a role model can be traumatic, prompt attention should be given to the entire congregation. The crisis transition plan should contain a list of mental health care providers, with contact names and phone numbers.

If the pastor has had a significant counseling ministry, those people will need immediate referral. Also, any person whom the pastor was assisting who was in crisis must be contacted and given additional resources. The crisis plan should address the confidentiality issues involved and furnish a list of referral sources.

Command Structure

In the emergency phase of a crisis (generally the first twenty-four hours but as long as one week), there is often insufficient time for collaborative or group decision making. Trusted individuals have to be given the authority to act. These individuals should be identified in the crisis plan.

Most critical is the designation of an acting head of staff. Because some decisions are time-critical, the designation should involve a primary as well as a secondary in case the former is not available. The plan should delineate the authority given to the acting head of staff and be communicated to the staff in advance so that they are prepared to comply with directives coming from that person.

It is generally helpful in the emergency phase of a crisis if one person can be authorized to act on behalf of the governing board. This may be the board chairperson, secretary, or personnel chairperson or other designee. Again, primary and secondary designations may be desirable.

Continuity of Service

Since the primary mission of the church is to provide service in the name of Christ, it is important that the plan feature a way for quality services to be continued wherever possible.

Certainly, the function of worship is critical to the strength, health, and healing of a congregation. The challenge is this: at the very moment when gifted preaching and worship leadership are most necessary, the primary resource available to the congregation has been removed. Here is where advance planning can help.

We recommend that before a crisis happens, certain steps should be taken. In conjunction with the pastor, decide which preacher(s) in the region (or nation) would be most effective in leading worship in an emergency situation. Your pastor should go to that preacher and have a conversation something like this: "None of us is immortal. It is poor shepherding of the Lord's people to leave the care of an entire congregation to chance. Here is the covenant I would like to make with you. In the event of a catastrophe that suddenly takes me from my pulpit, would you be willing to make the necessary changes in your plans so that you could lead worship in my church for two consecutive Sundays?"

Critical Pastoral Resource. We call this person your "CPR" (for critical pastoral resource). The purpose of a CPR is to offer worship leadership during those first two critical weeks when the right tone can have long-term benefits. This provision for a CPR in a crisis plan has a number of advantages. It gives the congregation a worship experience under the leadership of someone they know and trust. It brings a person with the right gifts to the situation that can promote healing and inspire confidence. It sends a clear signal to the congregation that the church is in capable and compassionate hands. Finally, it gives leaders who are working to provide interim worship leadership more time to do that task well.

Bridging Resources. The crisis plan should also provide a list of *bridging resources*. There are several categories. One is worship leadership. These are people who would be contacted to lead worship during the interim period before a new pastor can be called. This list should be developed in consultation with the pastor, since he or she is aware of good preachers in the region. Several sources should be considered. Large churches often have staff members who are excellent speakers but do not have regular worship responsibilities on Sunday morning. Many ministers who have a gift for speaking and have moved on to another career still would be available to lead worship on weekends. There are gifted lay speakers with a Christian commitment who can be found through local organizations such as toastmaster's clubs or service organizations.

A second category of bridging resources is pastoral and administrative. As with worship, the plan should define how administrative and pastoral responsibilities are to be handled. In some cases, the same person who provides worship leadership can also do the administrative and pastoral work. In other cases, the church may decide to segregate these responsibilities to get the best resources possible. After the list of possible bridging resources is constructed, primary and secondary designations should be made to reflect the best choices for the congregation.

In every case, these options should be explored in constructing the crisis plan *before they are needed*. This gives the church:

- More time to locate the best resources available
- An opportunity to get to know potential candidates for interim worship leadership
- Time to explore the parameters of availability (time of year, days and times of the week, duration of a possible commitment)
- An opportunity to negotiate terms of service in advance (compensation, reimbursement for expenses, contractual arrangements)

Regarding practical matters in the crisis plan, the pastor should provide clear guidance on how files should be handled, which are confidential and need to be destroyed, which should go to the successor, and which should enter the general church files. If the pastor's computer is protected by a global password, it may be best to give that keyword to a staff person; other personal documents can be protected by a personal password that does not need to be released. Arrangements should also be made regarding financial operations, including signing of checks and names on accounts. These things should all be covered in the plan.

Communication

One critical function in a crisis is communication. Generally, it is advisable that one person be given the responsibility for managing communication. There are a number of levels of communication that must be managed:

- Staff
- Lay leaders
- Congregation
- Area pastors
- Denominational bodies
- Friends of the church
- Geographical communities (local, regional, national)
- Media communities (radio, television, Internet)

Communication strategies should be consistent with the vision of the church and resonant with the culture that is being addressed. Where possible, contact should be established with local media so that a relationship can be established prior to a pastoral transition. The name of the communication manager along with contact information should be sent in writing to all television, radio, and newspaper reporters.

Staff members should be trained regarding communication in times of crisis, including an abrupt pastoral change. The plan should define what kinds of information they can release themselves and when they should refer those seeking information to the communication manager. In a situation where information must be released rapidly, phone trees managed by staff members can make every member of the church feel he or she is important while capitalizing upon the personal relationships of staff members to make communication feel less bureaucratic and more personal.

Restoration of Normalcy

Once the emergency phase of the crisis is past, work can be resumed on restoring the church to normalcy. This requires an orderly, focused process to recruit and orient a new pastor. The crisis plan must define the major elements of this process.

First, the leadership of the church confers with its search consultant to help shape the recruitment process. If the leaders choose to use a denominational or regional church resource, they should spend several hours laying out how the process will work, what resources will be provided, and what ecclesiastical rules must be observed. If the leadership is going to contract with a search consultant, then set up a similar meeting that also defines the contractual agreement between the consultant and the church.

Second, identify all the various players in the transition process and define their roles. Typically this includes the board members, the personnel chairperson, the consultant, the transition team, and the pastoral candidate.

Third, establish a realistic time frame for the work. Leaders and members alike need to know how long the process will take.

Fourth, define how the specifications for the new pastor will be established. If a strategic plan is not in place, it should describe how strategic targets are established. It should specify how the leadership identifies unique mission components (what you don't want to lose) and how it sets goals for the congregation's capacity and maturity (how strong you want to be). It should translate all this information into a description of what the new pastor should be prepared to do.

Fifth, specify how the new pastor will be oriented to his or her work, how *asset transfer* will take place, and what coaching or mentoring resources the new pastor might require.

Sixth, specify what spiritual resources are provided to leaders and members to assist them through this journey. A daily devotional guide for churches in pastoral transition is helpful.

It makes sense for the pastoral transition crisis plan to be the first step toward more general succession planning. Here are the reasons:

- The need for crisis planning in a church is not significantly different from the same need in any local organization. Schools, businesses, and libraries often have a crisis plan that can be a good model for a church to follow.
- Crisis planning for pastoral transitions is no-fault. It does not imply that the pastor is leaving soon, nor that the church wants it to happen. It is initiated by the reality that events occur over which we have little or no control.
- Crisis planning for a pastoral transition can help get people thinking strategically about a pastoral change and the need to do generic transition planning.
- Crisis planning for pastoral transition is inexpensive. It takes time to think through some critical issues, but there is generally no large outlay of money required.

Because a crisis plan has components that are relational in nature, with people playing various roles, it should be updated annually. In addition, because leaders change and memories grow hazy, the plan should be reviewed with staff and lay leaders every year as well. Copies of the plan should be made available to:

- Primary and secondary head of staff designee
- Primary and secondary board designee
- Personnel chair
- Communication manager
- CPR (the critical pastoral resource person)
- Transition consultant
- Primary and secondary bridging resources
- Regional religious bodies such as conferences or presbyteries
- Mental health referral sources

Chapter Fourteen

Getting Started on a Plan for Your Church

To everything there is a season, and a time to every purpose under heaven.

—Ecclesiastes 3:1 (NIV)

A journey of a thousand miles begins with the first step.

—Anonymous

There is an elephant in the board room. How do we begin to talk about it? A good starting point is to explore why we have not been talking about it all along. Most personal and organizational pathologies are the wisdom of a former time misapplied to the present. Only by honoring that former wisdom are we then freed to move forward to a wisdom that is appropriate for now.

It makes sense to avoid the issue of pastoral transition if the benefits are small and the penalties imposed by avoidance are not significant. In what kind of context does a surprise announcement from a departing pastor to a church with no transition plan have a relatively minor impact? Here are some descriptors:

- There is a surplus of pastors, and a high-quality successor will be readily available.
- The culture is favorably disposed to church involvement, and church membership is a standard expectation. The culture *pushes* people into the religious institution, and the church *pulls*

people toward itself. In times when the church is not functioning optimally (as in a transition), the push of the culture keeps
people involved.

 • There is a high degree of denominational loyalty. People
stay with a church even when it is not performing at a high level.

 • Off-the-shelf denominational programs are effective without significant localization or customization.

 • The culture has low expectations related to the quality or
scope of religious programming.

 • The culture has few competitors to the church for people's
time and resources.

In this environment, the downside of a pastoral transition is relatively small.

 The risks of broaching the subject in such an environment
are high. A pastor can be readily replaced and a conversation
about a pastoral transition might trigger a lame duck personnel
action that would not be positive; therefore he or she is not going
to raise the subject. Besides, pastors want to keep their options
open in systems that are fairly rigid. Their legacy is likely to be
captured in a building named after them, and the church is likely
to continue to grow after they are gone. If they continue to retirement they might receive emeritus status. Mobility is low, and it
is likely they can continue to have a relationship with members
who will probably stay in the same church for their entire lives.
Why rock the boat?

 Laypeople, on the other hand, risk disrupting a board meeting with matters extraneous to the normal board agenda. They
also risk the disfavor of regional governing bodies by flying in the
face of denominational policy and procedures that encourage
secrecy and one-size-fits-all thinking. In short, the elephant is
small, ignoring it has relatively minor consequences, and talking
about it is a distraction. There is wisdom in not talking about it.
Silence is the better part of valor.

Whether you are a pastor, a lay leader, or an entire board reading this book, acknowledge the value of the wisdom you inherited and the season during which it held sway.

Things have changed. Today, the elephant is large, ignoring it has major consequences, and talking about it holds out hope for a better church by sustaining the excellence that has been hard won over years of learning. A new wisdom is now needed.

Learning new wisdom for a new season is not easy. Patterns of thinking and behavior change slowly. Adult behavioral studies disclose to us that the best predictor of future behavior is past behavior. In other words, we know that the best predictor of whether someone will vote in the next election is not whether they *say* they will vote in the next election, but whether they voted in the *last* election. The reason that change is a spiritual issue is that without the resources of heaven it rarely happens.

Again, whether you are a pastor, a lay leader, or a board member it is important to acknowledge the anxiety that you may experience when moving into this uncharted water. Only by acknowledging this discomfort and facing it directly with the resources of prayer, study, and community will change really become possible.

If you are an older pastor, you may be avoiding retirement because you are anxious about what will happen to the church once you leave it.

If you are a middle-aged entrepreneurial pastor, you may be sure that you do not want to continue down the same path to retirement, but you are anxious about developing a succession plan.

If you are a layperson, you may be anxious about broaching the subject of a succession plan with a beloved pastor for fear of losing him or her.

Or you may be a layperson who believes that it is time for a pastoral transition, but you don't know how to initiate such a discussion without unintended consequences.

You may be a denominational official and you see all these situations but you are anxious about a misstep that would do more harm than good to the churches under your charge.

All the research is clear. A different cognitive understanding of an issue does not produce change. Only when a person or group of people are able to explore their fears in a safe environment does change become possible. In other words, change is first a spiritual issue before it is an informational one.

After we acknowledge the wisdom that brought us this far but now needs to be amended, and after we acknowledge our anxieties and fears, we need practical tools to begin to move forward. Again, the research shows that adults learn best when the information given them has immediate, practical application to something they care about. That's why Jesus didn't put his disciples into a class as He taught them. He took them on the road, where the needs were immediate.

The resources in this book should be a helpful way to move forward in addressing the issue of pastoral transition. When people see a practical way of moving forward, they are less likely to get stuck in denial and resistance. Faith is the organ of sight; hopelessness, the darkest blindfold.

Where a sea change is required in a culture, the workshop model is generally ineffective. The reason is that one individual is generally sent to the workshop and must return to market a set of ideas (that are countercultural) to an entire group of people who are stuck in a former wisdom, who have a bevy of anxieties, and who have no tools. Workshops hone skills and bolster confidence. They do not change cultures.

Therefore this subject should be broached with an entire group at one time. This can be done through a facilitated discussion that explores past wisdom, emotional and spiritual blocks, and the tools presented in this text. The discussion can be facilitated by the pastor, but we find this to be difficult in many cases. Here, the services of an outside consultant can be extremely valuable. Unfortunately, there are few consultants who are versed in the topic of pastoral transition. The authors stand ready to provide these services or may be able to give you a recommendation of someone in your area.

However you choose to address this issue, it is important that you do something as a starting point. A crisis transition plan (or a generic transition plan) can be a good first step. It does not require a timetable or negotiated planning. It does get leaders thinking about what a good transition might look like. After that step is taken, more comprehensive planning can take place that is more strategic and less contingency-driven.

The good news on this issue is that the leaders who need pastoral transition the most are also the most likely to consider innovative approaches to ministry. People who are developing creative ministry solutions know that these efforts are at risk during pastoral transition. But the very qualities of soul that give them their creative impetus lead them to consider alternatives to the outmoded thinking driving current transition models.

This is the way of Jesus. The Great Shepherd protects what He has brought into light from the womb of the Spirit. At its best, this is what transition planning is all about.

Appendix

The Church Planning Questionnaire: Catching a Vision of the Future

J. Russell Crabtree

This questionnaire can give the leadership of a church important baseline information on the health of a congregation prior to a pastoral transition. The data can guide the leadership in designing a transition plan that preserves strengths and manages vulnerabilities.

Administration of the Church Planning Questionnaire requires professional assistance. The general text is presented below to give a basic understanding of what is measured. For more information, contact the authors.

This questionnaire is designed to provide:

- A picture, through eighty-six standard questions, of what things are like in your church, such as:
- Five dimensions of church climate
    Warmth and support (items 25, 31, 36, and 39)
    Morale (items 6, 10, 18, and 40)
    Openness to change (items 8, 27, 33, and 15)
    Conflict management (items 3, 7, 13, and 34)
    Participation in decision making (items 12, 22, 32, and 41)

- Faith centrality (items 1, 5, 9, 35, and 43)
- Theological diversity (items 4, 14, 23, 29, 30, 38, 44, and 45)
- Views on educational process (items 16, 20, 21, 42, 44, and 47)
- The work of the pastor, given to him or her as a confidential document and covering worship and preaching (items 2, 28, and 37), pastoral care (items 11, 17, and 48), administration (items 19, 24, and 46), and community involvement (item 26)
- Goals for the future (priorities among sixteen are determined)
- Patterns of participation in church life, such as frequency of attendance, involvement in activity other than worship, giving, and so on
- Family demographics
- Relationships among items; for example, do people of various ages or length of membership see things differently in the church?

Compare your church with congregations of similar size on these items. Provide, through extra questions developed specifically for your congregation, the views of members on issues of particular concern to your situation.

The Church Planning Questionnaire

I. Your Personal Views and Beliefs

_____   1. It doesn't matter so much what I believe as long as I lead a moral life.

_____   2. Our pastor leads worship skillfully, involving the people in a meaningful way.

_____   3. There is a disturbing amount of conflict in our church.

_____   4. Spiritual matters, and not social or political affairs, should be the concern of the church.

_____   5. My religious beliefs are really the basis of my whole approach to life.

_____   6. It seems to me that we are just going through the motions of church activity. There isn't much excitement about it among our members.

_____   7. Problems between groups in this church are usually resolved through mutual effort.

_____   8. Our church changes its program from time to time to meet the changing needs of members.

_____   9. I experience the presence of God in my life.

_____ 10. The whole spirit in our church makes people want to get as involved as possible.

_____ 11. When conversing with a person, our pastor listens for feelings as well as words, and treats feelings as important.

_____ 12. The leaders of our church show a genuine concern to know what people are thinking when decisions need to be made.

_____ 13. Among most of our members there is a healthy tolerance of differing opinions and beliefs.

_____ 14. The stories in the Bible about Christ healing sick and lame persons by touch probably have a natural explanation.

_____ 15. Our church tends to stay very close to established ways of doing things.

_____ 16. Christian education takes place primarily in church school classes.

_____ 17. Our pastor has developed a good plan of visitation to members with special needs.

_____ 18. On the whole, members have a healthy pride in belonging to our church.

_____ 19. Our pastor helps develop opportunities for church leaders to receive training for their tasks.

_____ 20. The main purpose of Christian education is to help people learn to live as Christians in contemporary society.

_____ 21. The best Christian education programs are planned by the people who lead them and participate in them, rather than church publishers.

_____ 22. A small group of people seem to make most of the important decisions in our church.

_____ 23. Converting people to Christ must be the first step in creating a better society.

_____ 24. Our pastor is willing to spend extra time and effort to help a committee carry out a job in difficult circumstances.

_____ 25. A friendly atmosphere prevails among the members of our church.

_____ 26. Our pastor shows concern for community problems by working with others to help find solutions.

_____ 27. Our church tries to adapt its program to the changing needs of our community.

_____ 28. In preaching, our pastor consistently relates the message of Scripture to the needs of the people and the world.

_____ 29. People's behavior is determined primarily by the influences of society.

_____ 30. Scripture is the inspired Word of God, without error, not only in matters of faith but also in historical, geographical, and other secular matters.

_____ 31. I sense an atmosphere of genuine care and concern among our members in time of personal need.

_____ 32. In important decisions in our church, adequate opportunity for consideration of different approaches is usually provided.

_____ 33. On the whole, our people welcome new patterns or styles of worship.

_____ 34. There is frequently a small group of members who oppose what the majority want to do.

_____ 35. I try hard to carry my religion over into all my other dealings in life.

_____ 36. Strangers are usually made to feel welcome and at home in our church.

_____ 37. Our pastor preaches with a sense of conviction.

_____ 38. The primary purpose of people in this life is preparation for the next life.

_____ 39. People whose times of illness or special need are known by the members are assured of support in prayer.

_____ 40. On the whole, I am satisfied with how things are in our church.

_____ 41. People who serve on our church committees and board (council, vestry, session, and so on) represent a good cross-section of the membership.

_____ 42. I would rather be in a Christian education group where an informed leader uses most of the time to give a presentation than in one where members are led to study and share their ideas.

_____ 43. Although I believe in my religion, I feel there are other more important things in my life.

_____ 44. The main purpose of Christian education is to help people know what is in the Bible.

_____ 45. As I see it, Christianity should be clear about separating the spiritual and secular realms and putting emphasis on spiritual values.

_____ 46. Our pastor shows concern for the church's educational program.

_____ 47. Christian education is primarily for children and youths.

_____ 48. Our pastor does good work in counseling people with special problems.

II. *Priorities Among Goals*

_____ 49. Develop patterns of church worship that impart a stronger sense of God's presence.

_____ 50. Create a broader range of small groups for study or sharing life's experiences.

_____ 51. Provide a stronger program to increase financial support for the church's work.

_____ 52. Enlarge or improve the physical facilities of the church.

_____ 53. Establish a plan to enable new members to move more quickly into positions of church leadership.

_____ 54. Train a group of members to share with the pastor in visiting people who are ill or shut in, or who may have become inactive.

_____ 55. Establish a plan to enlist new members.

_____ 56. Strengthen the music program of the church.

_____ 57. Develop a stronger program for children and youths.

_____ 58. Develop a stronger program for young adults.

_____ 59. Develop a stronger program for adults.

_____ 60. Develop a stronger program for older adults.

_____ 61. Give more attention to relating the gospel to current social issues and community problems, providing opportunity for active involvement where feasible.

_____ 62. Strengthen patterns of pastoral care and counseling to help people deal with their problems, including training members to share in it.

_____ 63. Stimulate stronger support for the world mission of the church.

_____ 64. Implement a program of leadership development that enables people to receive education and training to perform their tasks well.

III. Participation in Church Life

_____ 65. On average, about how many times did you attend regularly scheduled church worship during the past twelve months?

_____ 66. Whether in this church or a former one, how does your present attendance in item 65 compare with *three years* ago?

_____ 67. Please indicate the degree of your participation during the past year in church activities other than worship, such as choir, church school class or similar study group, church committee or board, service or recreation group, and so on. Count the total of all such activities.

_____ 68. In relation to the activities in item 67, please indicate your agreement or disagreement with the statement, "On the whole, participation in church activities is very meaningful to me."

_____ 69. How many people do you know, at least by name and some personal contact, who are *not* members of your church but who come occasionally to worship or for some other activity?

_____ 70. Among your circle of friends, how many are members of your church?

_____ 71. How often do you find time for your own individual spiritual growth—that is, for prayer or the reading of Scripture and other materials related to faith?

_____ 72. How long have you been a voting or confirmed member of your present church?

_____ 73. Approximately how much do you contribute *individually* to your church per year? If you are married and you and your spouse contribute jointly, use the number beside *one-half* of that annual contribution.

IV. Individual Data

_____ 74. What is your gender?

_____ 75. What is your ethnic background?

_____ 76. What is your marital status?

_____ 77. What is your age range?

_____ 78. What is your highest level of education?

_____ 79. About how far is your residence from the church building?

V. Household Data

_____ 80. How many people are in your household? Please include yourself in the count.

_____ 81. How many children age five or under are in your household?

_____ 82. How many children age six to twelve are in your household?

_____ 83. How many youths age thirteen to eighteen are in your household? Include yourself if you are in this age group.

_____ 84. How many young adults age nineteen to twenty-four are in your household? Include yourself if you are in this age group.

_____ 85. How many adults age twenty-five or older are in your household? Again, include yourself, if you are in this group.

_____ 86. What is your household annual income range? If there is more than one wage earner or income from other sources, add all such sources for an approximate total. If you do not know the income range, enter your best estimate.

The Authors

Carolyn Weese and *Russ Crabtree* have been colleagues since 1987. Russ's analytical mind and survey tools coupled with Carolyn's intuitive insight and practical knowledge have proved to be instrumental in effective management and strategic planning for local churches across the United States.

As a pastor, Russ served in small, midsize, and large churches in New York and Ohio. His unique mix of gifts led him to working with churches, regional agencies, and nonprofit organizations in developing strategic planning. He has developed congregational assessment tools and has maintained a substantial database on church characteristics and congregations of all sizes and contexts. He has developed a number of products for churches in transition. Russ is a gifted teacher, preacher, trainer, and communicator. He is the founder and director of Holy Cow! Consulting.

Carolyn brings an extensive background in operational systems and know-how. Serving as a lay professional in an administrative position at First Presbyterian Church of Hollywood, California, gave her unique insight to the daily operation of a megachurch.

In an effort to assist churches in becoming more effective in fulfilling their vision, Carolyn formed Multi-Staff Ministries in 1984. Her work is based on solid Biblical principles and good business management practices. High-quality services to churches include overview of ministry; strategic, operational, and transition planning; staffing designs; stewardship models; congregational surveys; leadership development; and much more. A balance of good organizational tools and ingredients that build spirituality and leadership is the goal in a Multi-Staff consult. Multi-Staff Ministries has a proven track record of effectiveness in each of these areas. Carolyn is an effective communicator and conducts workshops and conferences. A Presbyterian Elder, she authored *Eagles in Tall Steeples: What Pastors and Congregations Wish They Knew About Each Other.*

Russ and Carolyn have joined hands in developing *The Elephant in the Board Room* in an effort to help churches bring change through healthy pastoral transition.

For further information, contact:

Multi-Staff Ministries
3819 N. 154th Lane
Goodyear, AZ 85338
Phone: 623-935-0747
CnHWeese@aol.com

Holy Cow! Consulting
P.O. Box 1805
Columbus, OH 43216
Phone: 614-291-8724
jrcrabtree@prodigy.net

Index

(NIV) identifies citations from the New International Version of the Holy Bible. The abbreviation (Exh.) indicates an Exhibit title. Topics annotated as (questions) are from the Church Planning Questionnaire Appendix.